Charles Steigerwalt

Catalogue of a $10,000 Collection of Choice United States and Foreign Coins, Paper Money, Medals, Etc.

No. 24

Charles Steigerwalt

Catalogue of a $10,000 Collection of Choice United States and Foreign Coins, Paper Money, Medals, Etc.
No. 24

ISBN/EAN: 9783742832498

Manufactured in Europe, USA, Canada, Australia, Japa

Cover: Foto ©Thomas Meinert / pixelio.de

Manufactured and distributed by brebook publishing software
(www.brebook.com)

Charles Steigerwalt

Catalogue of a $10,000 Collection of Choice United States and Foreign Coins, Paper Money, Medals, Etc.

CATALOGUE

OF A

$10,000 COLLECTION

OF

CHOICE UNITED STATES AND FOREIGN COINS, PAPER MONEY, MEDALS, ETC.

For Sale by CHAS. STEIGERWALT,

130 East King Street, Lancaster, Pa.

No. 24.　　　ESTABLISHED 1878.　　　FEBRUARY, 1891.

REMARKS.

Please Read. Send orders early to prevent disappointment. Do not order anything you have not a reasonable expectation of buying if found correct, and return anything not desired as soon as possible after receipt of goods. Some of the coins, etc., in this list are out on approval now, but are included, as they may be returned. Coins sent on approval to responsible buyers. Remittances should be made by Money Order, Postal Note, Registered Letter, Check or Draft. Don't send stamps of high values. Address all letters plainly, and make money orders, etc., payable to Chas. Steigerwalt, 130 East King Street, Lancaster, Pa.

Note. This collection is particularly choice, and is the largest ever offered for sale at fixed prices. It contains many gems, and all the rarities in the U. S. silver and copper series, except the 1804 dollar. The prices have been made low, as it is desired to clear the whole collection as soon as possible, that the amount realized may be invested elsewhere.

United States Gold.

1795. Eagle. Uncirculated. Proof surface. 25.00.
1797. Eagle. *Four stars facing.* About uncirculated. Semi-
   proof surface. Extra rare. 75.00.
1800. Eagle. Very nearly uncirculated. Brilliant lustre. 17.50.
1801. Eagle. Barely circulated. 12.50.
1804. Eagle. Uncirculated. Almost a strictly brilliant proof.
   Extra rare. 50.00.
1795. Half Eagle. Close date. *Proof.* 12.50.
1795. Half Eagle. Wide date. *Proof.* 12.50.
1796 over '95. Half Eagle. Very fine. 25.00.
1800. Half Eagle. Very fine. 6.00.
1802 over '01. Half Eagle. Uncirculated. 7.00.
1803. Half Eagle. About uncirculated. 6.50.
1804. Half Eagle. Very fine. 6.50.
1806. Half Eagle. Extremely fine. Lustre. 6.50.

1807. Half Eagle. Head to right. Extremely fine. Lustre. 6.50.
1810. Half Eagle. Uncirculated. 7.00.
1812. Half Eagle. Uncirculated. 7.00.
1813. Half Eagle. Uncirculated. 7.00.
1820. Half Eagle. Uncirculated. Semi-proof. 20.00.
1823. Half Eagle. Uncirculated. Brilliant mint lustre. 20.00.
1826. Half Eagle. Uncirculated. Very rare. 25.00.
1834. Half Eagle. *Old type.* Uncirculated. Bold impression.
   Brilliant mint lustre. 15.00.
1796. Quarter Eagle. Without stars. Fine. 20.00.
1797. Quarter Eagle. Very fine. 50.00.
1802. Quarter Eagle. About a brilliant proof. 12.50.
1804. Quarter Eagle. Barely circulated. 8.50.
1806 over '04. Quarter Eagle. Centre not well struck up (all
   that way), otherwise sharp impression. Brilliant mint
   lustre, semi-proof surface. Extremely rare. 50.00.

1806 over '05. Quarter Eagle. Extra fine. Excessively rare. 50.00.
1807. Quarter Eagle. Very fine. 7.50.
1808. Quarter Eagle. Fine. 6.00.
1824. Quarter Eagle. Barely if any circulated. 17.50.
1825. Quarter Eagle. Uncirculated. Semi-proof. 20.00.
1827. Quarter Eagle. Uncirculated. Brilliant mint lustre. 20.00.
1830. Quarter Eagle. Uncirculated. Semi-proof surface. 6.00.
1831. Quarter Eagle. *Brilliant proof.* 12.00.
1849. Dollar. Uncirculated. 2.00.
1850. Dollar. About uncirculated. 1.75.
1851. Dollar. Uncirculated. 1.75.
1852. Dollar. Uncirculated. 1.75.
1853. Dollar. Uncirculated. 1.75.
1854. Dollar. Small. Nearly uncirculated. 1.75.
1854. Dollar. Large. Uncirculated. 1.75.
1856. Dollar. About uncirculated. 1.75.
1857. Dollar. Extremely fine. 1.75.
1859. Dollar. Uncirculated. 2.00.
1862. Dollar. Uncirculated. 1.75.
1865. Dollar. Uncirculated. Semi-proof. 10.00.
1867. Dollar. Uncirculated. Semi-proof. 5.00.
1868. Dollar. Uncirculated. Semi-proof. 5.00.
1872. Dollar. *Proof.* 5.00.
1873. Dollar. Uncirculated. Brilliant. 2.00.
1874. Dollar. Uncirculated. Brilliant. 2.00.
1876. Dollar. *Brilliant proof.* 7.50.
1877. Dollar. *Proof.* 4.00.
1879. Dollar. Brilliant proof. 2.50.
1880. Dollar. Brilliant proof. 2.50.
1881. Dollar. Brilliant proof. 2.50.
1882. Dollar. Brilliant proof. 2.50.
1883. Dollar. Semi-proof. 2.00.
1884. Dollar. Semi-proof. 2.00.
1886. Dollar. Semi-proof. 2.00.
1887. Dollar. Brilliant proof. 2.50.
1888. Dollar. Semi-proof. 2.00.
1889. Dollar. Semi-proof. 2.00.
1849. Dollar. O. Mint. Barely circulated. 2.00.
1849. Dollar. D. Mint. Very fine. 3.00.
1851. Dollar. O. Mint. Barely circulated. 2.00.
1851. Dollar. C. Mint. Barely circulated. 3.00.
1852. Dollar. O. Mint. Extremely fine. 2.00.
1859. Dollar. C. Mint. Very fine. 3.00.
Georgia. "C. Bechtler at Rutherford, 5 Dollars." Rev., "Georgia Gold. 128 G. 22 carats." Semi-proof. 10.00.
Carolina. "A. Bechtler." Dollar. About uncirculated. 2.00.

United States Proof Sets.

1846.   Proof Set. Contains Dollar, Half Dollar, Quarter, Dime, Half Dime, and two Copper Cents (the tall 6 and the "Dutch 6." Half Cent lacking. The "Dutch 6" cent is sharp and perfect, but not as brilliant as proofs of late years, but the rest of the set is in nice condition. The Dime and Half Dime are beauties, and very rare in this condition. 90.00.

1856.   Proof Set. Contains Dollar, Half Dollar, Quarter, Dime, Three Cents, Copper Cent and Half Cent. Brilliant proofs. 50.00.

1857.   Proof Set. Similar to last. 50.00.

1858.   Proof Set. 7 pcs. 65.00.

1859.   Proof Set. 7 pcs. 6.00.

1860.   Proof Set. 7 pcs. 6.00.

1861.   Proof Set. 7 pcs. 6.00.

1862.   Proof Set. 7 pcs. 6.00.

1863.   Proof Set. 7 pcs. 6.00.

1864.   Proof Set. 9 pcs. 10.00.

1865.   Proof Set. 9 pcs. 8.00.

1866.   Proof Set. 10 pcs. 6.00.

1867.   Proof Set. 10 pcs. 6.00.

1868.   Proof Set. 10 pcs. 6.00.

1869.   Proof Set. 10 pcs. 5.00.

1871.   Proof Set. 10 pcs. 5.00.

1872.   Proof Set. 10 pcs. 5.00.

1873.   Proof Set. 10 pcs. 6.50.

1874.   Proof Set. 7 pcs. 5.00.

1877.   Proof Set. 8 pcs. 9.00.

1878.   Proof Set. Includes both dollars and the rare 20 cent. 6.00.

1879.   Proof Set. Both dollars. 4.00.

1880.   Proof Set. Both dollars. 4.00.

1881.   Proof Set. Both dollars. 4.50.

1882.   Proof Set. Both dollars. 4.50.

1883.   Proof Set. Both dollars. 4.50.

1884.   Proof Set. 4.00.

1885.   Proof Set. 4.00.

1886.   Proof Set. 4.00.

1887.   Proof Set. 4.00.

1888.   Proof Set. 4.00.

1890.   Proof Set. 3.50.

United States Dollars.

1794.   Very fine. An unusually even impression : stars, head and date well struck, as is also the reverse. 125.00.

1795.   Flowing hair. A beautiful specimen. Barely touched. Mint lustre. 15.00.

1795. Fillet head. Uncirculated. Proof surface. 75.00.
1795. Fillet head. Shows scarcely a trace of circulation. Sharp and with considerable lustre. 30.00.
1795. Fillet head. Almost equal to last. 20.00.
1796. Large date. Quite fine. 5.00.

1796. Small date. Very fine. 7.50.
1797. Seven stars facing. Very fine. 7.50.
1797. Six stars facing. Uncirculated. Brilliant mint lustre. 35.00.
1797. Six stars facing. Very fine. 7.50.
1798. Fifteen stars. *Small eagle.* Fine. 10.00.
1798. Thirteen stars. *Small eagle.* Very fine. 7.50.
1799. *Five stars facing.* Fine. 5.00.
1799 over '98. But little worn. 3.00.
1799. Strictly uncirculated. Brilliant mint bloom. 5.00.
1800. Barest touch of circulation. Brilliant mint bloom. 8.50.
1801. Very fine. Considerable lustre. 7.50.
1802. Barely touched on most prominent parts. Mint bloom. 10.00.
1802 over '01. Barely touched on most prominent parts. Mint lustre. 10.00.
1803. Could be called uncirculated. Sharp, handsome, with semi-proof surface. A beauty. 15.00.
1836. Brilliant proof. Sharp and handsome. 15.00.
1836. *Gobrecht in field.* Brilliant proof. 65.00. About uncirculated. Extremely rare. 40.00.
1838. *Brilliant proof.* 85.00.
1839. *Brilliant proof.* 60.00.
1840. Uncirculated. Proof surface. 3.50.
1841. Uncirculated. Mint bloom. Semi-proof. 3.00.
1842. Uncirculated. Mint bloom. 2.00.
1843. Uncirculated. Mint bloom. 2.00.
1844. Uncirculated. Handsome proof surface. 5.00.
1845. Uncirculated. Mint bloom. 5.00.
1846. Uncirculated. Mint bloom. 2.00.

1846.   O. Mint.   Barely touched.   Mint bloom.   Semi-proof sur-
        face.   3.50.
1847.   Uncirculated.   Mint bloom.   Semi-proof.   Handsome spec-
        imen.   3.00.
1848.   Uncirculated.   Semi-proof.   5.00.
1849.   Uncirculated.   Proof surface.   3.00.
1850.   *Brilliant proof.*   25.00.
1851.   *Brilliant proof.*   65.00.
1852.   *Brilliant proof.*   65.00.
1853.   Uncirculated.   Brilliant mint lustre.   5.00.
1854.   *Brilliant proof.*   30.00.
1855.   *Brilliant proof.*   25.00.
1857.   *Proof.*   A few stars not sharp.   6.00.
1858.   *Brilliant proof.*   60.00.
1859.   O. Mint.   Uncirculated.   Brilliant mint lustre.   2.50.
1860.   O. Mint.   Uncirculated.   Brilliant mint lustre.   3.00.
1865.   Dollar, half and quarter.   With legend " In God we Trust "
        above eagle on reverse.   Brilliant proofs.   Excessively
        rare.   Set for 75.00.

United States Half Dollars.

1794.   Very fine.   Bold impression.   Date strong.   8.00.
1795.   Uncirculated.   Mint lustre.   Planchet file marks.   10.00.
1796.   Sixteen stars.   Very fine and bold.   One of the best.
        125.00.

1796. Fifteen stars. Quite fine and a good companion to last. 75.00.

1797. Quite fine. 75.00.

1801. Extremely fine. Choice specimen. 15.00.

1802. Extremely fine. 15.00.

1805 over '04. Very fine. 7.50.

1806. *Proof.* 10.00.

1807. Head to right. A concave die has caused the head to wear, but otherwise the coin is uncirculated with brilliant mint bloom. 3.00.

1807. Head to left. About uncirculated. Sharp. 3.50.

1808 over '07. Barely touched. Mint lustre. 3.00.

1808. Perfect date. Uncirculated. Brilliant mint lustre. 4.00.

1809. Uncirculated. 2.00.

1810. Uncirculated. Brilliant mint lustre. Handsome. 3.00.

1811. Large date. Uncirculated. Brilliant mint lustre. 1.50.

1811. Small date. Brilliant mint lustre. Very sharp. 2.00.

1812. Uncirculated. Brilliant mint lustre. 1.50.

1813. Uncirculated. Brilliant mint lustre. 1.50.

1814. Uncirculated. Mint lustre. 1.50.

1815. Uncirculated. Semi-proof. One of the handsomest specimens of this date known. 25.00.

1815. Uncirculated. Sharp. 15.00.

1817. Uncirculated. Mint bloom. 2.00.

1818. *Proof.* 2.50.

1818 over '17. Uncirculated. Mint bloom. Sharp and handsome. 2.50.

1819. Uncirculated. Mint lustre. Sharp. 2.00.

1820. Small date. *Proof.* 3.50.

1820. Large date. Uncirculated. Brilliant mint lustre. 2.00.

1821. Uncirculated. Mint lustre. Sharp and handsome. 2.00.

1822. Uncirculated. Mint lustre. Sharp and handsome. 2.00.

1823. Uncirculated. Semi-proof. 2.00.

1824. Uncirculated. Mint lustre. Handsome. 1.50.

1824. Double profile. Uncirculated. Mint lustre. 1.50.

1825. Uncirculated. Mint lustre. Handsome. 1.50.

1826. Uncirculated. Proof impression. 3.50.

1827. *Proof.* 2.50.

1828. Plain 2. Small date. Uncirculated. Mint bloom. **Handsome.** 1.50.

1829. *Proof.* 2.00.

1829 over '21. Uncirculated. Mint lustre. 1.50.

1830. Uncirculated. Mint lustre. 1.00.

1831. Uncirculated. Mint lustre. 1.00.

1832. Uncirculated. Mint lustre. Semi-proof. Very handsome. 1.50.

1833. Uncirculated. Mint lustre. 1.00.

1834. Large date. Uncirculated. Mint lustre. 1.00.

8

1834. Small date. Uncirculated. Mint lustre. 1.00.
1835. Uncirculated. Mint lustre. 1.00.
1836. Uncirculated. Brilliant mint lustre. 1.00.
1836. Milled edge. Brilliant proof, a little haymarked. 15.00.
1836. Milled edge. Uncirculated. Brilliant mint lustre. 6.00.
1837. *Proof.* 2.50.
1838. Uncirculated. Mint lustre. 1.00.
1839. Head. Uncirculated. Mint lustre. 1.00.
1839. O. Mint. (O under head). Uncirculated. Brilliant mint lustre. 2.50.
1839. Liberty seated. *Without drapery from elbow to knee.* Uncirculated. 2.00.
1839. Liberty seated. *With drapery from elbow to knee.* Uncirculated. 2.00.
1840. Uncirculated. Mint lustre. Very handsome specimen. 2.00.
1841. Uncirculated. Mint lustre. Very handsome specimen. 2.00.
1841. O. Mint. Uncirculated. Mint lustre. 1.50.
1842. Large date. Uncirculated. Very handsome specimen. 1.50.
1842. Small date. *Proof impression.* 2.50.
1843. Uncirculated. Mint lustre. 1.00.
1843. O. Mint. Uncirculated. Mint lustre. 2.00.
1844. *Proof.* 4.00.
1844. O. Mint. Uncirculated. Mint lustre. Semi-proof. 3.00.
1845. O. Mint. Uncirculated. Mint lustre. 3.00.
1846. Uncirculated. Mint lustre. 1.00.
1847. Uncirculated. Mint lustre. 1.00.
1847. O. Mint. Uncirculated. Mint lustre. Slight proof surface. 2.50.
1848. Uncirculated. Mint lustre. 1.00.
1848. O. Mint. Uncirculated. Mint lustre. Sharp. 2.50.
1849. Uncirculated. Mint lustre. 1.00.
1849. *Brilliant proof.* 7.50.
1849. O. Mint. Uncirculated. Mint lustre. 2.00.
1850. Uncirculated. Mint lustre. 1.00.
1850. O. Mint. Uncirculated. Mint lustre. Handsome. 2.00.
1851. O. Mint. Uncirculated. Mint lustre. 2.50.
1851. P. Mint. Uncirculated. Mint lustre. 2.50.
1852. P. Mint. Uncirculated. Mint lustre. 6.00.
1852. O. Mint. *Proof impression.* 7.50.
1853. Uncirculated. Mint lustre. 1.00.
1854. *Brilliant proof.* 7.50.
1854. O. Mint. Uncirculated. Mint lustre. Semi-proof. 2.00.
1855. Uncirculated. Mint lustre. 1.00.
1855. O. Mint. Uncirculated. Mint lustre. 1.50.
1856. O. Mint. Uncirculated. Mint lustre. 1.50.
1858. Uncirculated. Mint lustre. Handsome, sharp specimen. 1.25.

United States Quarters.

1796. *Sharp proof*. Beautiful specimen. 75.00.
1796. Extremely fine, barely circulated. 20.00.
1804. Quite fine. Unusually bold. 15.00.
1805. Very fine and bold. 3.00.
1806   The centre of obverse and corresponding portion of **reverse** a little weak from weak die, otherwise uncirculated, brilliant mint lustre. 7.50.
1806 over '05. Fine and bold. 1.50.
1807. Fine and bold. 2.00.
1815. Small E above head. Uncirculated. Mint lustre. 3.00.
1818. Uncirculated. Mint lustre. 2.00.
1819. Barely circulated. Mint lustre. 2.00.
1820. Large O. *Proof*. 10.00.
1820. Small O. Semi-proof. Rare. 15.00.
1821. *Brilliant proof*. 7.50.
1821. Uncirculated. Mint lustre. 3.00.
1822. Uncirculated. Mint lustre. Handsome. 8.50.
1823. In good condition for this rare date, the date bold. 60.00.
1824. Quite fine. Rare so choice. 5.00.
1825. Uncirculated. Mint lustre. 3.00.
1827. *Brilliant proof*. 150.00.
1828. *Proof*. 7.50.
1828. Uncirculated. Mint lustre. 2.50.
1831. Uncirculated. Mint lustre. 1.00.
1832. Uncirculated. Mint lustre. 2.00.
1833. *Brilliant proof*. Very handsome and perfect. 20.00.
1834. Uncirculated. Mint lustre. 1.00.
1835. *Brilliant proof*. 10.00.
1835. Uncirculated. Mint lustre. 1.00.
1836. Uncirculated. Mint lustre. 1.50.
1837. *Proof*. 2.50.
1837. Uncirculated. Mint lustre. 1.00.
1839. Uncirculated. Mint lustre. 1.50.
1840. O. Mint. *No drapery from elbow to knee*. Uncirculated. Brilliant mint lustre. 3.50.
1840. O. Mint. *With drapery*. Uncirculated. Mint lustre. 2.50.
1840. P. Mint. *With drapery*. Semi-proof. 2.50.
1841. Uncirculated. Semi-proof surface. 2.50.

1842. O. Mint. Uncirculated. Mint lustre. 1.50.
1843. Uncirculated. Mint lustre. 1.25.
1844. O. Mint. About uncirculated. Mint lustre. 1.00.
1845. Uncirculated. Mint lustre. 1.25.
1846. *Brilliant proof*. 10.00.
1847. Uncirculated. Mint lustre. 1.00.
1849. *Brilliant proof*. 10.00.
1850. Uncirculated. Mint lustre. 1.50.
1852. Uncirculated. Mint lustre. 2.00.
1853. *Proof*. 2.50.
1853. *Without arrows or rays*. Uncirculated. Mint lustre. 15.00
1855. S. Mint. This mintage is extremely rare. Brilliant proof
    15.00.
1855. *Proof*. 2.00.
1856. *Brilliant proof*. 10.00.
1857. O. Mint. Uncirculated. Semi-proof. Handsome. 2.00.
1858. Brilliant proof. 2.00.

United States Twenty Cents.

1875. Brilliant proof. 1.00.
1876. Uncirculated. Brilliant mint lustre. .50.
1877. Brilliant proof. 3.00.
1878. Brilliant proof. 2.50.

United States Dimes.

1796. Cracked die. Uncirculated. Brilliant. 15.00.
1796. Perfect die. Uncirculated. Brilliant mint lustre. Very
    sharp and handsome. 20.00.
1797. Thirteen stars. Fine. 12.50.
1797. Sixteen stars. Very fine, but centre of reverse scratched
    12.50.
1798 over '97. 15 stars above eagle's head on reverse. Very fine.
    15.00.
1798 over '97. 13 stars above eagle's head on reverse. Very good.
    Very rare variety. 10.00.
1798. Perfect date. Except the stars to left, which are a little
    worn, the piece is almost uncirculated. Nice specimen.
    25.00.
1800. Could almost be called uncirculated. A beauty. 40.00.
1801. Barely touched by circulation. But for the fact that a pin
    scratch extends from top of hair to bottom of bust, would
    be one of the finest known. 12.50.

1802. Very good for date. 6.00.
1803. Extremely fine. In this condition exceedingly rare. 25.00.
1804. Quite fine and bold, nearly all the hair lines show. 35.00.
1805. Uncirculated. Brilliant mint lustre. 15.00.
1807. Barely touched. Brilliant mint lustre. 3 light scratches. 5.00.
1809. Quite fine and bold. 5.00.
1811. Quite fine and bold. 5.00.
1814. *Large date.* Uncirculated. Brilliant mint lustre. 7.50.
1814. *Small date.* Uncirculated. Brilliant mint lustre. Stars to right weak. Rare so fine. 7.50.
1820. Uncirculated. Large C in 10 C. Mint lustre. 5.00.
1820. Uncirculated. Mint lustre. Small C in 10 C. 5.00.
1821. *Large date. Brilliant proof.* 15.00.
1821. *Large date.* Uncirculated. Mint lustre. 3.00.
1821. *Small date.* Barely circulated. 2.50.
1822. But little worn. Mint lustre. 15.00.
1823. Uncirculated. Mint lustre. 12.50.
1825. *Brilliant proof. Sharp and perfect.* 20.00.
1827. *Brilliant proof.* 10.00.
1828. *Small date.* Uncirculated. Sharp. Brilliant mint lustre. Handsome specimen. 7.50.
1829. Uncirculated. Brilliant mint lustre. Very sharp and handsome. 2.50.
1830. *Brilliant proof.* 10.00.
1831. *Brilliant proof.* 10.00.
1832. *Proof.* Nick on edge. 2.00.
1833. Uncirculated. Mint lustre. 1.50.
1834. *Proof.* 3.00.
1835. *Brilliant proof.* Sharp and perfect. 10.00.
1836. Uncirculated. Mint lustre. 1.00.
1837. Head. Uncirculated. Mint lustre. 1.50.
1837. Liberty seated. Sharp brilliant proof. 12.50.
1838. *Without stars.* Uncirculated. Mint lustre. 10.00.
1838. *With stars.* Uncirculated. Mint lustre. 1.00.
1839. Uncirculated. Brilliant mint lustre. Sharp. 2.00.
1840. *Brilliant proof.* 5.00.
1841. Uncirculated. Mint lustre. 1.25.
1841. O. Mint. Uncirculated. Mint lustre. 1.50.
1842. Uncirculated. Mint lustre. Slight proof surface. 3.50.
1843. *Brilliant proof.* 10.00.
1843. Uncirculated Mint lustre. 1.25.
1845. Uncirculated. Mint lustre. 1.25.
1846. Uncirculated. 10.00.
1848. Uncirculated. Mint lustre. 3.00.
1849. *Brilliant proof.* 10.00.
1850. Uncirculated. Mint lustre. 1.25.
1851. Uncirculated. Mint lustre. 1.25.

1852. *Brilliant proof.* 7.50.
1852. Uncirculated. Mint lustre. 1.00.
1853. *Without arrows.* Uncirculated. Mint lustre. 1.50.
1853. *With arrows.* Proof. 2.50.
1853. *With arrows.* Uncirculated. Mint lustre. .75.
1854. O. Mint. Uncirculated. .75.
1855. *Brilliant proof.* 7.50.
1855. Uncirculated. Mint lustre. .50.
1856. *Large date.* Uncirculated. Mint lustre. 1.50.
1856. *Small date.* Uncirculated. Mint lustre. 1.25.
1856. *Small date.* O. Mint. Uncirculated. Mint lustre. Slight proof surface. 1.50.
1857. Uncirculated. Mint lustre. .50.
1857. O. Mint. Uncirculated. Mint lustre. 1.00.
1858. *Brilliant proof.* 2.00.
1858. Uncirculated. Mint lustre. Sharp, handsome specimen. .75.
1858. O. Mint. Uncirculated. Mint lustre. 1.00.
1859. O. Mint. Uncirculated. Mint lustre. 1.00.
1860. S. Mint. Uncirculated, brilliant mint lustre. Extremely rare in this condition. 15.00.

United States Half Dimes.

1794. Uncirculated with proof surface. A gem. 25.00.
1795. Uncirculated. Semi-proof. 12.50.
1796. Uncirculated. Brilliant mint lustre. Sharp impression. 35.00.

1796. Barely touched by circulation. Sharp and handsome. 20.00.
1797. *Fifteen stars.* Extremely fine. Sharp and handsome. 15.00.
1797. *Sixteen stars.* Uncirculated. Brilliant mint lustre. Sharp and handsome. 30.00.
1800. Very fine. 3.50.
1801. Shows but little circulation. One of the best of this date. 20.00.
1802. A good specimen of this extremely rare date. 100.00.
1803. Large S. Quite fine. Nearly all the hair lines show. 10.00.
1803. Small S. Extremely fine. Scarce variety. 15.00.
1805. Barest touch of circulation. Sharp and handsome. 35.00.
1829. Uncirculated. Mint lustre. .50.
1830. Uncirculated. Mint lustre. .50.

1831. *Brilliant proof.* 7.50.
1831. Uncirculated. Semi-proof. .75.
1832. Uncirculated. Semi-proof. .75.
1832. Knobbed 8. Uncirculated. Mint lustre. .75.
1833. Uncirculated. Mint lustre. .75.
1834. *Brilliant proof.* Trifling nick in field. 5.00.
1834. Uncirculated. Mint lustre. .75.
1835. Large date. Uncirculated. Mint lustre. .75.
1835. Small date. Brilliant proof. 7.50.
1835. Small date. Uncirculated. Mint lustre. .50.
1836. Uncirculated. Mint lustre. .75.
1837. *Head.* Uncirculated. Mint lustre. .75.
1837. *No stars. Curved date.* Brilliant proof. 7.50.
1837. *No stars. Curved date.* Uncirculated. Mint bloom.
       Sharp. Beautiful specimen. 2.50.
1837. *No stars. Straight date.* Uncirculated. Mint bloom. 1.50.
1838. *No stars.* Uncirculated. Brilliant mint bloom. Extremely
       rare in this condition. 15.00.
1838. *With stars.* Brilliant proof. 7.50.
1838. *With stars.* Uncirculated. Mint lustre. 1.00.
1839. *Proof.* 2.50.
1840. *With drapery. Fine proof.* 5.00.
1840. *Without drapery.* Uncirculated. Mint lustre. Semi-proof.
       1.50.
1841. Uncirculated. Mint lustre. 1.25.
1842. *Brilliant proof.* 12.50.
1842. Uncirculated. Mint lustre. Sharp. Slight proof surface.
       3.50.
1843. Uncirculated. Mint lustre. 1.00.
1844. P. Mint. Uncirculated. Mint lustre. Some proof surface.
       A beauty. 3.50.
1844. O. Mint. Uncirculated. 1.50.
1845. Uncirculated. Semi-proof. 2.00.
1846. Very fine. Very nice specimen of this scarce date. 7.50.
1847. *Brilliant proof.* 12.50.
1847. Uncirculated. Mint lustre. 1.00.
1848. *Large date.* Very fine. Rare so choice. 5.00.
1848. *Small date.* Obverse brilliant proof; rev., mint bloom. **A**
       beauty. 10.00.
1849. *Brilliant proof.* 10.00.
1849. Uncirculated. Mint lustre. Some proof surface. 1.50.
1850. P. and O. Mints. Uncirculated. Mint lustre. Sharp,
       handsome pair. 2.00.
1851. Uncirculated. Proof surface. 1.00.
1851. O. Mint. Uncirculated. Mint lustre. 1.00.
1852. Uncirculated. Mint lustre. .50.
1852. *Brilliant proof.* 7.50.
1853. *Without arrows.* Uncirculated. Mint lustre. 1.00.

1853. *With arrows.* Proof surface. 1.00.
1854. *Brilliant proof.* 7.50.
1854. Uncirculated. Mint lustre. .50.
1855. *Brilliant proof.* 7.50.
1855. Uncirculated. Mint lustre. .50.
1855. O. Mint. Uncirculated. Mint lustre. Some proof sur
     face. 1.50.
1856. *Brilliant proof.* 5.00.
1857. O. Mint. Uncirculated. Mint lustre. 1.00.
1858. *Brilliant proof.* 2.00.
1859. O. Mint. Uncirculated. Mint lustre. .25.
1859. *Reverse of 1860. Only two or three known. Semi-proof*
     20.00.
1860. *With stars. Proof.* 7.50.
1860. O. Mint. Uncirculated. Mint lustre. .75.

United States Silver Three Cents.

1851. Uncirculated. Mint lustre. Proof surface. 2.00.
1851. Uncirculated. Mint lustre. .50.
1851. O. Mint. Uncirculated. Mint lustre. .75.
1852. Uncirculated. Mint lustre. .50.
1853. Uncirculated. Mint lustre. .35.
1854. *Brilliant proof.* 7.50.
1854. Uncirculated. Mint lustre. 1.50.
1855. *Brilliant proof.* 7.50.
1855. Uncirculated. Mint lustre. 2.00.
1856. Uncirculated. Mint lustre. 1.50.
1857. Uncirculated. Mint lustre. .50.
1858. Brilliant proof. 2.00.
1858. Uncirculated. Mint lustre. .50.
1859. Brilliant proof. .50.
1862. Brilliant proof. .50.
1863. Brilliant proof. 1.00.
1864. Brilliant proof. 2.00.
1865. Brilliant proof. 1.50.
1866. Brilliant proof. 1.00.
1867. Brilliant proof. 1.00.
1868. Brilliant proof. 1.00.
1869. Brilliant proof. 1.50.
1870. Dull proof. .75.
1871. Uncirculated. Mint lustre. Semi-proof. .75.
1872. Brilliant proof. .75.
1873. Brilliant proof. 1.00.

United States Minor Coinage.

1856. Nickel Cent. Brilliant proof. 6.00.
1859. Nickel Cent. Brilliant proof. .50.
1861. Nickel Cent. Brilliant proof. 1.00.

1862. Nickel Cent. Brilliant proof. .40.
1863. Nickel Cent. Brilliant proof. .40.
1865. Bronze Cent. Brilliant proof, .50.
1869. Two Cents. Brilliant proof. .50.
1866. Five Cents. *With rays.* Brilliant proof. .50.
1866. Five Cents. *With rays.* Date separated by boll of shield. "In God we trust" smaller. *Brilliant proof.* Extremely rare. 3.50.
1866. Five Cents. *Without rays. Brilliant proof.* Extremely rare. 5.00.
1867. Five Cents. *With rays. Brilliant proof.* Rare. 3.50.
1877. Five Cents. Brilliant proof. 2.00.
1873. Minor proof set. 1, 2, 3, 5 cents. 1.75.
1877. Minor proof set. 1, 3, 5 cents. 4.00.
1878. Minor proof set. 1, 3, 5 cents. .75.

United States Cents.

1793. Chain "America." No periods after "Liberty" and date. The masses of hair slightly worn, otherwise about uncirculated. Light olive. 50.00.
1793. Chain "America." Periods after "Liberty" and date. Nearly uncirculated. Brown. 25.00.
1793. Wreath. Broad head and leaves. Small date. Very fine specimen. 12.50.
1793. Wreath. Stem of leaves over 7 and 9 of date. Very fine. Light color. 15.00.
1793. Wreath. Stem above 9 of date. Lettered edge. Fine. Light brown. 10.00.
1793. Liberty Cap. Very good. Beaded milling complete on both sides. Steel color. 12.50.
1794. Maris No. 3. "Sans Milling." Fine. Brown. 2.00.
1794. Maris No. 5. "Young Head." Fine. Brown. 2.00.

1794.   Maris No. 11.   " Many Haired." Nearly fine. Brown. 1.50.
1794.   Maris No. 12.   " Scarred Head." Extremely fine. Light
        olive. 12.50.
1794.   Maris No. 13.   "Standless 4." Very fine. Brown. 3.50.
1794.   Maris No. 14.   " Abrupt Hair." Only touched on the
        masses of hair. Light olive. 12.50.
1794.   Maris No. 20.   " Fallen 4." Very fine. Brown. 4.00.
1794.   Maris No. 21.   " Short Bust." Very fine. Chocolate. 3.50.
1794.   Maris No. 25.   " The Ornate." Very fine. Steel color. 3.50.
1794.   Maris No. 26.   " Amiable Face." Very fine. Light brown.
        3.50.
1794.   Maris·No. 28.   " Large Planchet." Extremely fine, light
        olive, but depressed on cheek and neck. 2.00.
1794.   Maris No. 29.   " Marred Field." Fine. Light olive. 2.50.
1794.   Maris No. 32.   " Shielded Hair." About fine. Brown. 2.00.
1794.   Maris No. 36.   " The Plica." Nearly fine. Brown. 2.00.
1794.   Maris No. 38.   " Roman Plica." Fine. Light brown. 2.50.
1794.   Maris No. 39.   " 1795 Head." Quite fine. Dark olive. 3.50.
1794.   Maris No. 40.   " Many Haired." Fine. Light brown. 2.50.
1794.   Maris No. 42.   "Trephined Head." About fine. 2.00.
1794.   Maris No. 45.   Good. Rare. 1.50.
1794.   Maris No. 46.   Very fine. Hair but little worn. 5.00.
1794.   Maris No. 50.   Fine. 3.00.
1795.   Lettered Edge.   Fractional mark regular. One berry on
        each side of ribbon bow. Uncirculated. Light olive. $5.00.
1795.   Lettered Edge.   Fractional mark irregular. Berry on left
        of ribbon bow, none on right. Extremely fine. Brown.
        20.00.
1795.   Thick planchet, but unlettered edge. Barely circulated.
        Brown. 10.00.
1795.   Thin Planchet, " One Cent " in center of wreath. Uncir-
        culated. Beautiful glossy light olive. A splendid cent.
        35.00.
1795.   Thin Planchet. " One Cent " high in wreath. Uncircu-
        lated. Light olive with traces of original red. A few
        letters are a little weakly struck, otherwise a splendid
        specimen. 20.00.
1796.   Liberty Cap. Wide date. Very fine. 7.50.
1796.   Fillet Head. Uncirculated. Brown. 20.00.
1796.   Fillet Head. . Broken die. Fine. Brown. 3.50.
1797.   Uncirculated. Red. 20.00.
1797.   Break in die back of head near ribbon bow. Uncirculated
        Brown. 15.00.
1797.   Break in die back of head near bottom of hair. Uncircu-
        lated. Brown. 15.00.
1798.   Large date. Extremely fine. Brown. 5.00.
1799.   Fine for date. The date particularly fine and well struck
        Desirable specimen. 35.00.

1799 over '98.　Very good specimen of this variety.　Light brown
　　20.00.
1800　over '99.　Extremely fine.　Hair lines scarcely touched.
　　Good color.　5.00.
1800.　Perfect date.　Broken die.　Extremely fine.　Brown.　5.00.
1801.　The curious variety with wrinkles before face.　Uncircu-
　　lated　Partly bright red.　20.00.
1801.　The hair lines scarcely touched.　Olive-brown.　Only defect
　　a slight discoloration in obverse field.　8.00.
1802.　Uncirculated.　Beautiful light olive.　5.00.
1802.　No stems to wreath.　Very fine.　Brown.　3.00.
1802.　Die broken below date.　Barely touched.　Handsome olive.
　　3.00.
1803.　Large 1-100.　Barest circulation.　Handsome light olive.
　　3.00.
1803.　Small 1-100.　Uncirculated.　Traces of brightness.　5.00.
1803.　Die broken below date.　But little circulated.　Brown.　2.00.
1804.　Broken die.　Fine for date.　15.00.
1804.　Perfect die.　Very good, date sharp.　12.00.
1805.　Uncirculated.　Beautiful glossy light brown.　20.00.
1806.　Barely circulated.　Steel color.　25.00.
1807.　Perfect date.　About uncirculated.　Handsome purple
　　brown.　7.50.
1807.　Perfect date.　Comet variety.　Very fine.　Light olive.
　　5.00.
1807 over '06.　Fine.　Light olive.　4.00.

1808.　Scarcely circulated, but a light impression.　Light olive.
　　10.00.
1808　12 star variety (so-called).　Very fine and sharp.　Brown.
　　5.00.
1809.　Uncirculated.　Dark olive.　25.00.
1810.　Perfect date.　Barely circulated.　Light olive.　7.50.
1810 over '09.　Extremely fine.　Steel color.　5.00.
1811.　Perfect date.　Quite fine.　Brown.　5.00.
1812.　Large date.　Uncirculated.　Beautiful light olive.　20.00.
1812.　Small date.　Barely circulated.　Olive-brown.　5.00.
1813.　Scarcely a trace of circulation, if any.　Sharp impression.
　　Handsome steel color.　7.50.

1814. Plain 4. Uncirculated. Light olive. 7.50.
1814. Plain 4. Double chin. Barely circulated. Light olive. 5.00.
1814. Cross 4. Uncirculated. Unusually sharp. Handsome steel color. 7.50.
1816. Perfect die. Uncirculated. Brilliant red. 3.00.
1816. Broken die. Uncirculated. Brilliant red. 2.00.
1817. Point of tiara between stars, wide date. Uncirculated. Bright red. 1.50.
1817. Star near point of tiara. Uncirculated. Obverse, reddish-olive; reverse, brilliant red. Unusually sharp impression, broad milling. 2.50.
1817. Fifteen stars. Extremely fine. Glossy light brown. 3.00.
1818. Uncirculated. Brilliant red. .50.
1819. Small date. Uncirculated. Brilliant red. Very sharp semi-proof impression. 3.00.
1819 over '18. Uncirculated. Partly bright. A few stars weak, and spot of discoloration on reverse. 1.00.
1820. Perfect date. 2 with large curl. Uncirculated. Brilliant red. 3.00.
1820. Uncirculated. Brilliant red. 1.00.
1820 over '19. Uncirculated. Beautiful light olive with traces of original red. 6.00.
1821. Not much circulated. Glossy steel color. 7.50.
1822. Uncirculated or barely touched. Glossy light olive. 7.50.
1823 over '22. Very fine. Glossy brown. 5.00.
1824. Uncirculated. Red and iridescent. Handsome specimen. 25.00.
1825. Sharp, perfect, beautiful impression. Uncirculated. Handsome even reddish olive. 20.00.
1826. Uncirculated. *Brilliant red.* 15.00.
1827. *Brilliant red proof.* 25.00.
1828. Large date. Barely circulated. Very light olive. 7.50.
1828. Small date. Fine or very fine. Bold. 6.00.
1829. *Proof impression.* Light olive with traces of red. 15.00.
1830. Small date. Sharp impression, sharp milling. Barely circulated. Beautiful purple color. 5.00.
1830. Large date. Barely circulated. Orange color. 5.00.
1831. Large letters in legend. Uncirculated. Brilliant red. 10.00.
1831. Small letters in legend. *Brilliant red proof.* 20.00.
1832. Uncirculated. Reddish olive. 10.00.
1833. Date near milling. Uncirculated. Brilliant red. 10.00.
1833. Date near head. Uncirculated. Beautiful purple brown. A gem. 5.00.
1834. Small date. Uncirculated. Handsome light olive. 5.00.
1835. Barely circulated. Handsome light olive. 5.00.
1836. Perfect die. Uncirculated. Light olive. 5.00.
1836. Die broken to left. Uncirculated. Glossy reddish brown. 5.00.

1836. Die broken to right. Uncirculated. Brown. 5.00.
1837. Beaded hair-string. Uncirculated. Brilliant red. 5.00.
1837. Plain hair-string. Uncirculated. Brilliant red. 3.00.
1838. *Brilliant proof.* 12.50.
1838. Uncirculated. Brilliant red. 3.00.
1839. Head of 1838. Barely circulated. Greenish-olive. 3.00.
1839. Booby Head. Uncirculated. Glossy light olive. 5.00.
1839. Silly Head. Fine. Purple-brown. 1.50.
1839. Head of 1840. Extremely fine. Light brown with traces of red. 3.00.
1839 over '36. Very good. Better than usually found. 4.00.
1840. Large date. Uncirculated. Partly bright. 7.50.
1840. Small date. *Brilliant proof.* 12.50.
1840. Small date. Barest touch of circulation. Glossy light brown. 3.00.
1840. Small date. Doubly cut date. Barely circulated. Glossy light brown. 3.00.
1841. *Brilliant proof.* 20.00.
1842. Large date. Uncirculated. Light olive. 2.00.
1842. Small date. Extremely fine. Light brown. 2.00.
1843. Obverse and reverse of 1842. *Brilliant proof.* 20.00.
1843. Obverse and reverse of 1842. Uncirculated. Brilliant red. 10.00.
1843. Obverse of 1842 and reverse of 1844. Uncirculated. Glossy chocolate color. Almost proof surface. 7.50.
1844. *Brilliant proof.* 20.00.
1844. Uncirculated. Beautiful glossy olive brown. 3.00.
1845. Uncirculated. Reddish. 2.00.
1846. Sharp, perfect proof, but not as brilliant as some of the other proofs. 10.00.
1846. Uncirculated. Brilliant red. 3.00.
1847. Uncirculated. Brilliant red. 3.00.
1848. *Brilliant proof.* 10.00.
1848. Uncirculated. Brilliant red. 3.00.
1849. *Brilliant proof.* 15.00.
1849. Uncirculated. Brilliant red. 2.00.
1850. *Brilliant proof.* 12.50.
1850. Uncirculated. Brilliant red. Beautiful specimen. Semi-proof. 1.50.
1851. Uncirculated. Brilliant red. Beautiful clean specimen. 1.00.
1852. Uncirculated. Brilliant red. Beautiful clean sharp specimen, with some proof surface. 1.50.
1853. Uncirculated. Brilliant red. Clean specimen. .75.
1854. Uncirculated. Brilliant red. Clean specimen. 1.00.
1855. Slanting 5's. *Brilliant proof.* 7.50.
1855. Straight 5's. Uncirculated. Brilliant red. Beautiful clean specimen. Semi proof surface. 1.25.
1856. Slanting 5. Uncirculated. Brilliant red. Nice specimen. .75.

1856. Straight 5. Uncirculated. Brilliant red. .75.
1857. Small date. *Brilliant proof.* Sharp and perfect. 7.50.
1857. Small date. Uncirculated. Brilliant red. 1.50.
1857. Large date. Uncirculated. Brilliant red. 2.00.

United States Half Cents.

1793. Uncirculated. Glossy brown. 15.00.
1794. Date close to bust. Uncirculated. Glossy dark brown. 10.00.
1794. Date distant from bust. Extremely fine. Glossy light brown. 5.00.
1795. Lettered edge. About uncirculated. Light olive. 12.50.
1795. Lettered edge. Comma between 1 and 7 of date. Very fine. Glossy light brown. 5.00.
1795. Thin planchet. Uncirculated. Handsome surface. 15.00.
1795. Thin planchet. Comma between 1 and 7 of date. Uncirculated. Light olive. 15.00.
1797. Date close to head. About uncirculated. 6.00.
1797. Date distant from head. Fine. Brown. Broad milling. 3.00.
1797. *Lettered edge.* Very good. Rare variety. 7.50.
1800. Extra fine. Light color. 1.50.
1802. Fine. Rare in this condition. 5.00.
1803. Uncirculated. Beautiful light olive. 3.00.
1804. Plain 4. Uncirculated. Handsome light olive. 1.50.
1804. Crossed 4. Uncirculated. Light olive. 1.50.
1805. With stems to wreath. Uncirculated. Light olive. 4.00.
1805. No stems to wreath. Uncirculated. Light olive. 4.00.
1806. Large date. Uncirculated. Brilliant red. 1.50.
1806. Small date. No stems to wreath. Extremely fine. Light olive. 1.00.
1807. Uncirculated or barely touched. Light olive. 3.00.
1809. Uncirculated. Handsome color. 2.50.
1810. Uncirculated. Brown. 5.00.
1811. Fine and bold. 3.00.
1825. Uncirculated. Beautiful iridescent light olive. 2.00.
1826. Uncirculated. Beautiful light olive. 1.50.
1828. 12 stars. Uncirculated. Glossy light olive. 1.50.
1828. 13 stars. Uncirculated. Brilliant red. 2.00.
1829. Uncirculated. Brilliant red. 2.00.
1832. Uncirculated. Brilliant red. 2.00.

1833. *Brilliant proof.* 5.00.
1834. *Proof.* 3.50.
1834. Uncirculated. Brilliant red. 2.00.
1835. Semi-proof. Brilliant red. 2.50.
1840. Large berries on reverse. *Brilliant proof.* 17.50.
1841. Large berries on reverse. *Brilliant proof.* 17.50.
1841. Small berries on reverse. *Brilliant proof.* 12.50.
1843. Small berries on reverse. *Brilliant proof.* 12.50.
1844. Small berries on reverse. *Brilliant proof.* 12.50.
1847. Small berries on reverse. *Brilliant proof.* 15.00.
1849. *Small date. Brilliant proof.* 15.00.
1849. Uncirculated. Mint lustre. 1.50.
1850. *Brilliant proof.* 5.00.
1851. *Brilliant proof.* 5.00.
1851. Uncirculated. Mint lustre. .75.
1852. *Brilliant proof.* 12.50.
1853. Uncirculated. Mint lustre. .75.
1854. *Brilliant proof.* 5.00.
1855. *Brilliant proof.* 3.50.
1856. *Brilliant proof.* 3.50.
1857. *Brilliant proof.* 3.50.

Washington Coins.

1783. "Unity States" Cent. Very fine. Light olive. .75.
1783. Large head. "United States" Cent. Fine. Brown. .75.
1783. Small head. "United States" Cent. *Engrilled edge.* Very
    rare variety. Very fine. 2.50.
Double-head Cent. Uncirculated. Glossy light brown. 2.50.
1789. Cent. Obv., head of Washington. "Geo. Washington
    born Virginia, Feb. 11, 1732." Rev., "Gen. of the Amer-
    ican Armies, 1775: Resigned 1783: President of the
    United States, 1789." Very fine. Brown. Rare thus. 7.50.
1791. Cent. Large eagle. *Brilliant proof.* 6.00.
1791. Cent. Small eagle. Very fine. 5.00.

1792. Silver Half Dollar. "G. Washington President I. 1792."
    Very good specimen of this rare coin, but a small hole
    above head has been skillfully plugged. 50.00.

1792. Cent. Very good. Brown. 12.50.

1792. Cent. " Washington President 1792." The rare variety
       with one star above eagle's head. Extra fine, light brown
       color. Marred a little by several nicks on obverse. 40.00

1793. Half-penny, rev., ship. Extra fine. Olive brown. 3.00.

Liberty and Security. Large size. Edge lettered : " An asylum for
       the oppress'd of all nations." Uncirculated. Bright. 3.50

Liberty and Security. Small size. About uncirculated. Glossy
       brown. 2.50.

North Wales Token. Fine for piece. 1.50.

Success to U. S. Large and small sizes. Barely circulated. Nice
       pair. 2.50.

Funeral Medal. Reverse, skull and cross-bones. Pierced at top
       as usual. Silver. Good. Size 18. Rare. 5.00.

American Colonials.

SILVER.

Maryland. Lord Baltimore Shilling, Sixpence and Fourpence
       The Shilling is fine and bold, the Sixpence very good and
       the Fourpence fine but a little weak at right of obverse
       and corresponding reverse. The set is very desirable
       Set for 75.00.

1783. Chalmers Annapolis Shilling. Extremely fine. 12.50.

1783. Chalmers Annapolis Sixpence. Very good. 12.50.

1783. Chalmers Annapolis Threepence. Extremely fine. A lit-
       tle beauty. 17.50.

1652. Massachusetts Pine Tree Shilling. Very broad planchet
       Extremely fine. 15.00.

1652. Massachusetts Pine Tree Sixpence. Very fine. 10.00.

1652. Massachusetts Pine Tree Shilling. Small planchet. Very
       fine. 8.00.

New Jersey. St. Patrick Shilling : dragons and serpents flying
       and dying from the saint's presence : church to right.

Rev., King David with harp. Two light nicks, otherwise
nearly fine. Very rare. 15.00.

COPPER.

Rosa Americana Twopence. Plain rose. Variety without date.
Uncirculated. Light olive color. A beauty. 7.50.

1722. Rosa Americana Penny. Plain rose. Uncirculated. 5.00.

1723. Rosa Americana Penny. Crowned rose. Uncirculated.
5.00.

1723. Rosa Americana Penny. Vtile Dulci. Very rare variety.
Extremely fine. 7.50.

1766. Pitt Token. "No stamps." About uncirculated. Glossy
light olive. A beauty. 5.00.

1766. Pitt Token. Same as last, but appears to have been struck
in pewter or a composition containing a considerable
portion of that metal. About uncirculated. 5.00.

1776. Continental Currency. Tin Dollar. 2 R's in "Currency."
Very fine 10.00.

1776. Continental Currency. Tin Dollar. The rare variety with
only one R in "Currency." Extremely fine. 12.50.

1785. Vermonts Res Publica. Unusually good and bold. 5.00.

1786. Vermontensium. Very fine. Light brown. 3.00.

1786. Auctori Vermon. Baby head. Fine for piece. 3 00.

1785. Vermon Auctori. Rev., "Immune Columbia." Always
poor—this about as usually found. 5.00.

1787. Massachusetts Cent. Horned bust. Extremely fine. Olive color. 2.50.

1788. Massachusetts Cent. Uncirculated. Light brown. 3.00.

1787. Massachusetts Half Cent. Uncirculated. Light olive. 3.50.

1788. Massachusetts Half Cent. Uncirculated. Partly bright. 3.50.

1787. Connecticut Cent. Horned Bust. Very fine. 1.00.

1787. Connecticut Cent. "Auctori *Connect.*" Last part of "Auctori" and corresponding reverse weak, otherwise uncirculated. Light brown. 1.00.

1786. Auctori Plebis. Plain bust. I. C. under head. Rev., "Hispanola." Large legends. Very good. Rare. 1.50.

1786. Auctori Plebis. Draped bust. Rev., "Hispanola." Small legends. Fine. Light color. 2.00.

1786. Auctori Plebis. Draped bust. Larger legend. Reverse seems to be plain or extremely weakly struck. Fine. 1.50.

1786. New York Cent. Bust of Washington. "Non Vi Virtute Vici." Rev., Liberty seated. "Neo-Eboracensis." Very fine. Brown. 50.00.

1787. New York Cent. "Liber Natus Libertatem Defendo." Indian with tomahawk and bow. Rev., eagle standing on section of globe. "Neo-Eboracus 1787 Excelsior." Uncirculated, with traces of red. Trifling planchet defect on edge. Excessively rare. 125.00.

1787. New York Cent. "Liber Natus Libertatem Defendo." Indian with tomahawk and bow. Rev., Arms of New York, "Excelsior" below. Very good or fine excepting that a small hole at Indian's feet has been plugged. Extremely rare. 25.00.

1787. New York Cent. Arms of New York, "Excelsior" below; rev., eagle. Very good. 20.00.

1787. Nova Eborac. Seated figure to right. Very fine. Light brown. 4.00.

1787. Nova Eborac. Seated figure to left. Fine. 3.00.

1787. Nova Eborac. The extremely rare variety with two quatrefoils before "Nova." Nearly fine. Light brown. 10.00.

1794. Talbot, Allum & Lee. John Howard reverse. Very fine. Brown. 1.50.

1795. Talbot, Allum & Lee. Uncirculated. Light olive. 2.00.

Kentucky Cent. Thin planchet. Uncirculated. 2.00.

Kentucky Cent. Lettered edge. Uncirculated. Glossy olive. Semi-proof surface. 3.00.

1787. Immunis Columbia. Liberty seated on globe. Fine. Light color. 6.00.

1787. Franklin Cent. "Mind your business." Rev., "States United." Uncirculated. Bright red. .75.

1787. Franklin Cent. Same, but reverse, "United States." Un-

circulated. Bright red. Planchet a little defective. Rare.
1.25.

New Jersey. St. Patrick Halfpence ("Mark Newby"). St. Patrick showing shamrock to people. Large and small letters
in legend. Fine pair. Brown color. Pair for 8.00.

New Jersey. St. Patrick Farthings. St. Patrick banishing the
snakes from Ireland. Fine specimens from 7 different
dies. Set of 7 pieces for 10.00.

New Jersey. "1786. Immunis Columbia" obverse with New
Jersey reverse. Maris 3-C. Only 6 known. Barely circulated. Handsome olive. 85.00.

1786. New Jersey. 12-G. *No coulter*. A light impression, but
really uncirculated. Light olive with traces of red. 5.00.

1786. New Jersey. 12-I. *No coulter*. Good. Rare. 3.00.

1788. New Jersey. 50-f. Horse head to left. Very fine. 5.00.

1773. Virginia Half Cent. Uncirculated. Brilliant red. .75.

North Carolina Token (so-called). Ship; rev., shield, 13 stars.
Brass. Uncirculated. 1.25.

1783. Nova Constellatio. Almost uncirculated. 1.00.

1783. Nova Constellatio (sic). Club rays. Extremely fine.
Brown. 1.00.

1785. Nova Constellatio. Very fine. Olive color. 1.00.

James II. Tin Plantation Piece. Pewter. Barely circulated.
2.50.

United States Patterns.

1792. Disme. Silver. Fine. Only one other known in silver,
and the date is rubbed off of that piece. 125.00.

1792. Martha Washington Half Disme. Uncirculated. Semiproof. A beautiful specimen. 25.00.

1792. Silver-Centre Cent. Head of Liberty facing to right.
LIBERTY PARENT OF SCIENCE & INDUSTRY.
Rev., ONE CENT in wreath, $\frac{1}{100}$ below. UNITED

STATES OF AMERICA. This specimen is struck on
a full copper planchet—no hole for silver centre—and is
rarer than the silver centre specimens. I know of no
duplicate. Barely circulated. Dark olive. 100.00.

1838. Half Dollar. Liberty seated. Rev., flying eagle. Silver
proof. 25.00.

1838. Half Dollar. Head of Liberty. Rev., flying eagle. Silver,
nearly proof. 4.00.

1838. Half Dollar. Head of Liberty. Rev., standing eagle. Silver proof. 7.50.

1839. Half Dollar. Nude bust of Liberty facing to *right*. Reverse same as regular issue of 1839–1841. Silver proof.
35.00.

1839. Half Dollar. Same as last, but with reverse of 1842–1865.
Silver proof. 35.00.

———. Pattern 3 Cents. "3;" rev., III. Nickel. Uncirculated.
1.00.

1850. Three Cents. Liberty cap in rays. Brilliant proof. 3.50.

1850. Ring Cent. No hole; rev., blank. Silver alloy. .75.

1853. Cent. Liberty head. Nickel. Dull proof. 1.00.

———. Blank obverse. Reverse same as last. Nickel proof. .50.

1854. Cent. Head of Liberty without stars. Bronze proof. .75.

1855. Cent. Flying eagle. Bronze proof. .75.

(1856). Flying eagle. No date or legend. Copper proof. 2.00.

1857. Cent. Head of Liberty; rev., "One Cent" in wreath.
Nickel proof. 3.00.

1858. Half Dollar. Obverse of regular issue. Reverse, Paquette's
design with motto-ribbon in eagle's beak. Silver. Dull
proof. 20.00.

1858. Quarter Dollar. Obverse of regular issue. Reverse, Paquette's design—no ribbon. Silver proof. 15.00.

1858. Cents. Set of twelve patterns. Indian head, large and
small eagles, each with four reverses. 10.00.

1858. Cent. Indian head. Nickel proof. 1.00.

1859. Liberty Head. Reverses, "½ dollar," "Half dollar," "50
cents"—also, Liberty seated. Silver proofs. Set of 4
pieces for 6.00.

1859. Quarter Dollar. Obverse of regular issue. Reverse,
Paquette's design—no motto-ribbon. Silver proof. 7.50.

1859. Cent. Regular issue; rev., oak wreath and shield. Uncirculated. 1.00.

1861. Half Dollar. Rev's., "God our Trust" in field above eagle
on reverse, and "God our Trust" on label. Brilliant
proofs. Pair for 7.50.

1862. Half Dollar. Rev's., "God our Trust" in field above eagle
on reverse, and "God our Trust" on label. Brilliant
proofs. Pair for 5.00.

1863. Half Dollar. Rev's., "God our Trust" in field above eagle on reverse, and "**God** our Trust" on label. Brilliant proofs. Pair for 7.50.

Ten Cents. Postage Currency. Silver proof. 1.00.

Pattern Three Cents. Obverse **same as** old copper cent; rev., 3 cents in wreath. Copper proof. 2.50.

Pattern Three Cents. Same as last. **Aluminum proof.** 5.00.

Pattern **Two Cents.** Head of Washington. **Rev.,** similar to regular issue, but "Cents" more curved. Aluminum proof. 3.00.

Pattern Two Cents. Same as **last, but thinner planchet.** Aluminum proof. 3.00.

Pattern Two Cents. Same as **last. Nickel proof. 3.00.**

Pattern **Two Cents.** Same as last. Copper proof. 1.50.

Pattern **Two Cents.** Similar to issue of 1864, but with reverse like last, "Cents" curved. Copper proof. 1.50.

Pattern Two Cents. Same as last, but thin planchet. Copper proof. 1.50.

Pattern Two Cents. Same as last. Nickel proof. 3.00.

Cent. Thin planchet. Copper proof. 1.00.

Quarter Dollar. Obverse of regular issue. Rev., smaller eagle with long arrows. Silver proof. 7.50.

Two Cents. Regular issue, but in an alloy containing a large proportion of nickel. Proof. 1.50.

Cent. Obverse of regular type; reverse is obverse of 1858 eagle cent, small legend. Nickel proof. 5.00.

Quarter Dollar. Obverse of regular issue. Rev., smaller eagle with long arrows. Silver proof. 7.50.

Five Cents. Type adopted in 1867—no bars. Nickel proof. Extremely rare. 15.00.

Two Cents. Regular issue, but in an alloy containing a large proportion of nickel. Proof. 1.50.

Cent. Pure nickel. Uncirculated. 1.50.

Cent. Milled edge. Copper proof. 1.50.

Five Cents. Head of Lincoln. Rev., Value in wreath. Nickel proof. 20.00.

Five Cents. Head of Lincoln. Copper proof. 10.00.

Five Cents. Head of Washington, "In God we Trust." Rev., 5 in wreath. Nickel proof. 1.50.

Five Cents. Obv., same as last; rev., same as regular issue. Nickel proof. 1.50.

Five Cents. Obverse same as regular issue. Reverse, large 5 in wreath. Nickel proof. 1.50.

Five Cents. Same as last, but small 5 in wreath. Nickel proof. 1.50.

Five Cents. Obverse same as regular issue except that the date is separated by a boll; reverse, 5 in wreath. Nickel proof. 1.50.

1867.   Five Cents.   Head of Liberty.   Rev., " 5 cents" in wreath "Cents" straight.   Nickel proof.   .75.

1867.   Five Cents.   Same as last, but "Cents" curved.   Nickel proof.   .75.

1867.   Cent.   Pure nickel.   Uncirculated.   1.50.

1867.   Five Cents.   Longacre's design.   Profile to left with long plumes.   Rev., V. on shield.   Aluminum proof.   Rare.   1.50.

1868.   Ten Cents.   Obverse same as old copper cent.   Nickel proof.   5.00.

1868.   Ten Cents.   Same as last.   Copper proof.   2.50.

1868.   One, Three, Five Cents.   Liberty head.   Nickel proofs.   2.00.

1869.   50, 25, and 10 Cents.   Draped head of Liberty, with Phrygian cap; another bust with plain diadem; another with star on forehead.   Three of each value.   Reeded edges.   Silver proofs.   Set of 9 pieces.   7.50.

1869.   Similar set.   Aluminum proofs.   5.00.

1869.   Three Cents.   Nickel.   Dull proof.   .50.

1870.   50, 25, and 10 Cents.   Draped head of Liberty, with Phrygian cap; another bust with plain diadem; another with star on forehead.   Three of each value.   " Standard " in small letters on reverse.   Reeded edges.   Silver proofs.   Set of 9 pieces.   7.50.

1870.   Similar set.   Aluminum proofs.   5.00.

1870.   Similar set but " Standard Silver " in large letters.   Silver proofs.   10.00.

1870.   Similar to last.   Aluminum proofs.   7.50.

1870.   Longacre's Dollar.   Indian queen.   Silver proof.   20.00.

1870.   Barber's beautiful patterns.   Liberty seated with shield, and pole with cap.   Values on reverse in figures within a wreath of cotton, corn and sugar.   " Standard" above.   Plain edges. $1, 50c., 25c., 10c., 5c.   Silver proofs.   Set for 40.00.

1870.   Same.   Reeded edge except the 5 and 10 cents.   Copper proofs.   7.50.

1870.   Same.   Plain edges.   Copper proofs.   7.50.

1870.   Same, including a 3 cent piece.   Reverse same as the regular issue.   Reeded edges, except the dollar.   Copper proofs.   7.50.

1870.   Same as last.   Dollar, half, quarter and dime.   All plain edges.   Copper proofs.   5.00.

1871.   Longacre's dollar, half, quarter, dime and half dime.   Indian queen.   Rev., 1 Dollar, etc., " Standard" above.   Silver proofs.   The dollar excessively rare.   Set 50.00.

1871.   Five Cents.   Head of Liberty.   Rev., " V Cents " in wreath.   Nickel proof.   2.00.

1873.   Set of the six rare pattern Trade Dollars.   Splendid proofs.   30.00.

1874.   Twenty Cents.   Female seated on globe.   Silver proof.   20.00.

1874. Twenty Cents. Female seated on globe. Copper proof. 5.00.
1875. Twenty Cents. Female seated on globe, holds olive branch, steamship at sea. Silver proof. 12.50.
1875. Twenty Cents. Head of Liberty; reverse, "20" on shield. Silver proof. 12.50.
1875. Twenty Cents. Same as regular issue, but with reverse "½ of a dollar." Silver proof. 12.50.
1877. Half Dollars. Head of Liberty in circle of pellets, "E Plurius Unum" above, date below, 7 stars to right, 6 to left. Reverses of Maris sale, Nos. 198, 199, 200. Copper proofs. 3 pcs. 7.50.
1877. Half Dollar. Head of Liberty with broad band inscribed "Liberty." 13 stars. Rev., Maris sale No. 204. Small eagle on large shield. Copper proof. 2.50.
1878. Goloid Metric Dollar. Brilliant proof. 10.00.
1878. Barber's beautiful pattern for the Standard Dollar. The rejected design, which was handsomer than the one by Morgan accepted. Also, the original Morgan design with only 3 leaves to branch under eagle's feet. Brilliant proofs. Pair for 15.00.
1879. Double Eagle. Has "30 G. 1.5 S. 3.5 C. 35 grams 1879," separated by stars on obverse around Liberty head; rev., same as regular issue. Gold proof. Only 3 struck. 100.00.
1879. Silver metric and goloid dollars. Brilliant proofs. Pair for 4.00.
1881. One, Three. Five Cents. Obverse similar to adopted designs; rev., value in Roman numerals in corn and oak wreath. Nickel proofs. 3.50.
1882. Five Cents. Obverse and reverse same as regular issue without "Cents," excepting in date. Nickel proof. 3.50.
1882. Five Cents. "United States of America" around head. Reverse, V in corn and oak wreath, "E Pluribus Unum" above. Nickel proof. 3.50.
1882. Five Cents. "In God we trust," above Liberty head. Reverse same as issue without "Cents." Nickel proof. 3.50.
1882. Same as the regular issue of this year (old design), except that the shield on reverse is large and has no boll at bottom. Extremely rare. Nickel proof. 5.00.
1883. Five Cents. Same as the regular issue, excepting a band inscribed "Cents" on reverse over V. Nickel proof. 3.5.0
1883. Five Cents. Same as regular issue without "Cents," but has word "Liberty" above head on obverse. Nickel proof. 3.50.
1883. Five Cents. Obverse, Liberty head surrounded by "United States of America." Reverses have a wreath of corn, cotton and sugar surrounded by 13 stars, 6 to right, 7 to left, "Five" above, "Cents" below. In the center is the per-

centage of metal: " 50 N. 50 C.," " 33 N. 67 C.," and
" Pure Nickel." Nickel proofs. *Only 3 sets struck.* Two
of these are in prominent collections. Set of 3 pieces
25.00.

Confederate Notes.

$100. 1861. Montgomery. Train of cars to right. Fine. 10.00
$100. 1861. Richmond. Train of cars to left. Uncirculated
15.00.
$50. 1861. Montgomery. Negroes hoeing cotton. Uncircu
lated. 7.50.
1864. Set from 50 cts. to $500. 1.25.

Foreign Crowns and Multiples of Crowns.

(All of crown size unless otherwise stated.)

Austria. 1549. Ferdinand I. Fine. 3.50.
1558. Ferdinand I. With title as Duke of Burgundy. Fine. 3.50.
1592. Rudolph II. Extremely fine. 3.00.
1603. Maximilian. As Grand Master of Teutonic Knights. Uncirculated. 3.50.
1610. Rudolph II. Very fine. 3.00.
1612. Mathias II. Uncirculated. 3.50.
1617. Ferdinand II. Very fine. 2.50.
1621. Leopold. Uncirculated. Brilliant mint lustre. 3.50.
1631. Ferdinand II. Broad Crown. Fine. 2.50.
——. Archduke Ferdinand Charles. *Double Crown.* Extremely
fine. 6.50.
1638. Ferdinand III. Extremely fine. 2.50.
1640. Ferdinand III. *Double Crown.* Uncirculated. 7.50.
1656. Ferdinand III. Fine. 2.50.
1660. Leopold. Very fine. 2.50.
——. Leopold and Claudia de Medici. *Double Crown.* Uncirculated. Brilliant mint lustre. 7.50.
1683. Broad Sede-Vacante Crown. Double-headed eagle on world,
crescent in clouds. Barely circulated. 3.00.
1690. Leopold the Hogmouth. Broad Crown. Extremely fine.
2.50.
1701. Leopold the Hogmouth. Uncirculated. 3.00.
Augsburg. 1625. Ferdinand II. Saint above pine cone. Uncirculated. Brilliant mint lustre. 3.50.
1643. Ferdinand III. View of city and pine cone on reverse.
Uncirculated. Brilliant mint lustre. 3.50.
Brandenburg. 1549. Albert. Fine. 3.50.
Brunswick. 1562. Henry. Rev., arms supported by a wild man.
Fine. Rare. 5.00.
(15)78. Eric. Shield before wild man is surrounded by the order
of the Golden Fleece. Fine. Very rare. 5.00.
1597. Henry Julius. " Truth " Crown. Scene of crucifixion,
"Veritas" above. Fine. 3.00.

99. Henry Julius. "Wasp" Crown. Lion and wasps. Very fine. 5.00.

—. Augustus. "Ship" Crown. Uncirculated. 5.00.

24. Christian. Uncirculated. 3.50.

40. Frederick. Gothic inscriptions. Very good. 2.50.

43. Augustus. "Bell" Crown. Three hands pulling bell. "*Ano.* 1643." Very fine. 3.50.

43. Augustus. "Bell" Crown. "*Ao.* 1643." Fine. 3.00.

62. Christian. "Horse" Crown. Fine. 3.50.

85. Rudolph Augustus. *Broad Triple Crown.* Female playing the lute, standing on a snail, mining scene and landscape in distance. Uncirculated. 30.00.

87 Ernest Augustus. ⅔ Crown. Wild man. Uncirculated. Rare. 3.50.

88. Rudolph Augustus and Anton Ulrich. Busts jugata. *Broad Crown.* About uncirculated. 4.00.

16. Augustus William. Wild man holding pine tree. Fine. 3.00.

asle. Broad Double Crown. View of the city. Extremely fine. 6.50.

rabant. 1567. Extremely fine. 3.50.

22. Philip IV. Fine. 2.50.

58. Philip IV. Very fine. 2.50.

avaria. 1625. Maximilian. Virgin and Child. Rev., Arms of the Palatinate. Extremely fine. 2.50.

ampen. 1597. Date between turrets of castle. Very good. 2.50.

enmark. 1659. Frederick III. Sword dividing hand, date Feb. 2nd. Extremely fine. Very rare. 3.50.

enoa. 1631. Conrad II. (King of the Romans). Broad 1½ Crown. Very fine. Rare. 5.00.

65. Thick Double Crown. Fine. 4.00.

87. Virgin and Child. Broad Double Crown. Small hole at top. Very fine. 3.50.

amburg. 1600–1700. Marriage Triple Crown. Man and woman, hands joined. Extremely fine. 10.00.

00–1700. Broad Baptismal Double Crown. Scene of Baptism in Jordan. Extremely fine. 5.00.

ungary. 1556. Ferd. I. Very fine. 3.50.

olland. 1682. *Triple Crown.* Knight on horseback. Uncirculated. Brilliant mint lustre. 10.00.

esse. 1631. "Whirlwind" Crown. Fine. 3.50.

uneberg. 1548. Profile in Crescent. Fine. Very rare. 5.00.

antua. Charles I. Rev., Sun progressing through signs of Zodiac, stars in field, world below. Extremely fine. Rare. 5.00.

ansfield. 1624. Wolfgang John George. Very good. 2.00.

etherlands. 1790. Insurrection Crown. Lion with sword and shield. Proof. 4.00.

oland. 1727. Frederick Augustus. Mortuary ⅔ Crown. In

honor of Christina, Queen of Poland. Cypress between pyramid of hearts. Fine. 2.00.

Parma. 1627. Odoardo Farnese. Rev., bust of St. Antonius as a Roman soldier. Extremely fine. 3.00.

1631. Odoardo Farnese. Rev., St. Antonius carrying standard. Uncirculated. 3.50.

Presburg. 1716. Wolfgang. Uncirculated. 2.50.

Russia. 1762. Peter III. Only reigned 6 months. Very good. 3.00.

Salzburg. 1552. Michael. Very fine. 3.50.

1593. *Square Double Crown.* Four heads blowing wind against a tower. Fine. 7.50.

1621. St. Rupert seated. Uncirculated. Mint lustre. 3.00.

1628. Two bishops holding up cathedral; rev., procession of priests carrying religious emblems. Very fine. 3.00.

1630. Uncirculated. Brilliant mint lustre. 3.00.

1708. John Ernest. Uncirculated. Brilliant mint lustre. 2.50.

St. Gall. 1624. "Bear Crown." Fine. 3.00.

Schaffhausen. 1621. Ram springing from temple door. Very good. 2.50.

Schwarzenberg. 1696. Ferdinand and Maria Anna. Busts jugata. Very fine. 2.50.

Spain. 1558. Philip of Spain, with title as King of Spain and England. Fine. 3.50.

Sweden. 1632. Gustavus Adolphus. About uncirculated. Rare. 4.00.

1718. Charles XII. "Med Gutz heilp." Very fine. Rare. 2.50.

Saxony. 1537. John Fred. and George. Very fine. 3.50.

1540. John Fred.; rev., bust of Henry. Nearly uncirculated. 4.00.

1583. John and Fred. Wm. Bust on each side. Good. 2.50.

1593. "Three Dukes." Quarter Crown. Fine. 1.00.

1598. "Three Dukes" Crown. Very fine. 3.00.

1602. John Casimer and John Ernest. Busts facing. Barely circulated. 3.00.

1606. Christian II. with drawn sword; rev., busts of John George and Augustus facing. Very fine. 2.50.

1615. John George. Square Double Crown. Fine. 6.00.

1620. "Four Dukes" Crown. Three busts in procession; rev., bust. Uncirculated. 3.50.

1624. Busts of Wm., Fred. and Fred. Ernest. Barely circulated. 3.50.

1625. John George. Bust with drawn sword. Barely circulated. 3.50.

1630. John George. Half crown, Crown and Double Crown. Centennial of Augsburg Confession. An almost uncirculated set. 12.50.

1635. John George. Fine. 2.50

1652. John George. Uncirculated. Mint lustre. 3.50.

1661. John George II. Broad Double Crown (over 2½ in. in diameter). Monument. To left; open book, crowned, with snake on cross and Christ on cross—to right; crossed swords and cap. Uncirculated. A beauty. 15.00.

Sicily. 1732. Charles III. *Triple Crown.* Bust with curls to right. Rev., Phoenix. Uncirculated. Brilliant mint lustre. 15.00.

Transylvania. 1591. Three boar tusks on reverse. Uncirculated. 3.50.

Tuscany. 1665. Ferdinand II. Rev., rose bush. Fine. Rare. 3.00.

1671. Max. Henry. Nearly uncirculated. Mint lustre. 3.00.

1676. Cosmos III. Rev., Baptism in Jordan. Fine. 2.50.

Venice. John Cornaro I. (1625–1630.) Lion of St. Mark on shield. Very good. 2.50.

1683. Aloysius Contarino, Doge. St. Martin and the beggar. Exceedingly fine. Size 23. 3.00.

Paolo Renier. (1779–1789). Dollar. Doge with standard kneeling before St. Mark. Rev., Lion before castle. Uncirculated. 3.50.

Wittenberg. 1661. Reformation Crown. Bust of Luther; rev., view of the city. Nearly uncirculated. Rare. 4.00.

West India Society. (Dutch.) Monogram of the Company, surrounded by the crowned shields of the United Provinces. Rev., view of fort and ship. Extremely fine and rare. 7.50.

Werda, Suabia. 1543. Charles V. of Austria. W. on shield on reverse for Werda. Fine. 3.50.

West Frisia. 1596. *Double Crown.* Neptune on sea monster. Very good. 6.00.

1601. Lions. *Double Crown.* Uncirculated. 10.00.

Zug. 1621. Extremely fine. 3.50.

Zealand. 1642. Very good. 2.50.

1664. ⅗ Crown. Crowned eagle with bunch of arrows; rev., sun (IHS in centre) and crescent. Extremely fine. Rare. 3.00.

Silver Siege and Necessity Coins.

Breda. 1625. Diamond shape. Size 14. Very fine. 2.50.

Carthagena. 1873. 2 and 5 Pesetas. Struck while the Centralists besieged the city. Uncirculated. Very rare. Pair for 6.00.

Gotha. 1567. Siege crown. Very fine. 3.50.

Haarlem. 1572. Oblong. Size 16x20. Fine. Very rare. 4.00.

Majorca. 1821. Ferd. VII. Siege Dollar. Uncirculated. 3.00.

Mozambique. Oblong square Onza of 6 Cruzados (Dollar); M and three counterstamps; rev., ONCA in octagon: 2 counterstamps. Very rare and odd. 4.00.

Middleburg. 1572. Square Siege Crown. Extremely fine. 5.00.

Munster. 1660. Square Siege Crown. Extremely fine. 5.00.

Minden. 1624. Oblong Siege Coin for 8 Groschen. Very fine. 2.00.

Nurnberg. 1650. Diamond-shaped Peace Klippe. Hand with wreath over globe. Uncirculated. Size 20. 2.50.

Saragossa. 1809. Ferd. VII. Siege Dollar. Uncirculated. 3.00.

Salzburg. 1651, 1656. Klippes (diamond shaped) for one-sixth and one-ninth Crown. Very fine. Pair, 2.50.

Jewish Coins.

Simon Maccabeus. B. C. 143. Half Shekel. Cup of manna; rev., a triple lily or hyacinth. Very fine, but slight erosion on obverse. 15.00.

John Hyrancus. B. C. 136. *Widow's Mite.* Good. Very rare. 2.50.

Alexander Jannæus. B. C. 78. *Widow's Mite.* Good. 2.00.

Alexander II. B. C. 49. *Widow's Mite.* Fine, but reverse misstruck. 2.00.

Under Roman Procurator. A. D. 14. *Widow's Mite.* Date palm. Good. 2.00.

Herod Agrippa II. A. D. 37. (The Herod the King of Acts xii. 1.) *Mite.* Wheat heads and royal umbrella. Fine. 2.00.

Claudius Felix, Procurator under Nero. *Mite.* A palm branch; rev., wreath. Very good, but edge nicked. 1.50.

Vespasian. A. D. 70. Denarius. Rev., captive beside armor, "Judæa" below. Struck to commemorate the destruction of Jerusalem. The finest specimen I have seen in a long time. 6.00. Another, fine. 3.00.

Vespasian. A. D. 70. Great bronze. Rev., captive under tree, soldier watching, "Judæa Capta." Very good. 7.50.

Vespasian. A. D. 70. Great bronze. "Judæa Devicta." Obverse very good; rev., poor, but shows figure, shield and part of legend. 1.00.

Roman Bronze, etc.

Aes. Early type. B. C. 500. Double head of Janus; rev., prow. Weight 9 oz. Very good. 7.50.

Quadrans. Early type. Boar on each side. Fine. 2.50.

Sextans. Early type. Head of Minerva; rev., prow. Fine. 2.50.

Aes. Reduced type. Double head of Janus; rev., prow. Fine. 1.50.
Semis. Reduced type. Head of Jupiter; rev., prow. Very fine. 1.00.
Egypt. Large Bronze. Head of Jupiter; rev., eagle. Fine. Size 28. Weigh
    3¼ oz. 2.50.
Egypt. Similar. Size 25. Fine. Weight 1¼ oz. 1.50.
Turkuman. Youluk-Arslan. A. D. 1180. Khalefeh, squatted, holds sword up
    lifted in right hand and male head in left. Fine. 1.25.
Youluk-Arslan. A. D. 1180. Bust facing in square. Fine. 1.00.
Ortokides Dynasty. Golbeddin el Ghazi. A. D. 1176. Large and small busts
    rev., cuneiform characters. Fine. 1.00.
Mahmoud Benu Zengee. A. D. 1223. Head facing. Fine. 1.00.
Similar to last. Caliphs of Bagdad. Heads and squatting figures. Good to fine
    one pierced. 7 pcs. 2.50.
Herculaneum. Lead coins from ruins. As usually found. 8 pcs. 2.00.
Augustus and Agrippa. Rev., crocodile chained to palm tree. COL. NEM. (Colony
    Nemausus). Very fine. 2.00.
Nerva. A. D. 96. G. Bronze. Very good. 1.25.
Balbinus. A. D. 238. G. Bronze. Good. Very rare. 2.50.

Roman Silver Denarii.

Pompey the Great. Born 106 B. C. Head between lituus and vase. Very good
    3.50.
M. Junius Brutus. Head of Liberty; rev., trophy, BRUTUS IMP. Very fine. 3.00
M. Junius Brutus. Head, "Libertas." Rev., procession of lictors, BRUTUS below
    Very fine. 2.50.
Julius Cæsar. Struck about 47 B. C. Head of Ceres. "Cos Tert Dict Iter."
    (Consul third time; Dictator second time). Rev., pontifical implements
    Extremely fine. 3.50.
Julius Cæsar. "Cæsar Dict. Perpetuo." Veiled head of Cæsar; rev., Venus Ni
    cephore standing holding a victory and hasta. Very good. 2.50.
Julius Cæsar. Head of Venus to right; rev., two Gaulish captives under a trophy
    "Cæsar" below. Uncirculated. 3.50.
Julius Cæsar. Laureated head of Apollo; rev., prætor drawing two oxen. "IMI
    CÆSAR." Very fine. 3.50.
Julius Cæsar. Elephant trampling a serpent; rev., religious implements. Uncir
    culated. Brilliant mint lustre. 2.50.
Mark Anthony. War galley; rev., standards, LEG V. Good. .75.
Augustus Cæsar. B. C. 31. Youthful head. "C. Cæsar III." Uncirculated
    3.00.
Galba. A. D. 68. Good. 1.00.
Vitellius. A. D. 69. Fine and rare. 3.00.
Vespasian. A. D. 70. Extremely fine. 1.50.
Titus. A. D. 79. Very good. Scarce. 1.50.
Domitian. A. D. 81. Fine. 1.00.
Nerva. A. D. 96. Very good. 1.00.
Trajan. A. D. 98. Extremely fine. 1.50.
Hadrian. A. D. 117. *Double Denarius.* Very good. Rare. 2.00.
Hadrian. A. D. 117. Rev., star and crescent. Very good. 1.00.
Antonius Pius. A. D. 138. Very fine. 1.00.
Septimus Severus. A. D. 193. Barely circulated. 1.00.
Geta. A. D. 211. Fine. .75.
Elagabalus. A. D. 218. About uncirculated. 1.00.
Severus Alexander. A. D. 222. Extremely fine. 1.00.
Philip the Arab. A. D. 244. Extremely fine. .75.

Ancient Greek Coins.

Tetradrachms. Athens. Archaic style. 525 B. C. Head of Athena; rev., owl
    Very fine. 5.00.

Macedonia. Philip III. **Type of Alexander the Great.** Very good but test cut on edge. 2.00.

Alexander the Great. 336 B. C. *As it dropped from the die.* The sharpest and handsomest specimen I have seen. 15.00. Another, very good. 3.50.

Macedonia as a Roman province. 158 B. C. Shield, centre of which is bust of Artemis; rev., club in wreath. Obv., fair; rev., fine. 1.50.

Same. 89 B. C. Head of Alexander the Great with flowing hair and Ammon horn, "Macedon" below. Rev., club, money chest and chair in wreath, with name of the Roman Quæstor Aesillas. Very fine. 5 00.

Side, Pamphylia. 190 B. C. Fine helmeted head; rev., winged Nike with wreath. Very fine. 5.00.

Syracuse. 400 B. C. Head of Arethusa surrounded by dolphins. Rev., Victory in biga. Very good. 4.00.

Thrace. 323 B. C. King Lysimachus. Head of the deified Alexander with Ammon horn. Rev., Pallas Nicephorus seated. Fine. 5.00.

Thrace. 146 B. C. Head of the young Dionysos; rev., Hercules with club. Very broad planchet, rude design. Very fine. 2.50.

Tyre. 126 B. C. Head of Hercules; rev., eagle. Fine. 5.00.

Egypt. One of the earlier Ptolemies. Very good. 3.50.

Ptolemy XIII. 79 B. C. Fine. 3.50.

Didrachms. Aegina. Earliest period. 700 B. C. Turtle; rev., punch marks. Fine. 5.00.

Agrigentum. 472 B. C. Sea eagle and crab. Very fine. 2.50. Another, larger eagle and crab. Good. 1.00.

Bœotia. 379 B. C. Shield; rev., amphora. Very good. 2.50.

Chios. 500 B. C. Seated griffin; rev., punch marks. Fine. 4.00.

Caulonia. 480 B. C. Nude slinger and stag; rev., stag. Fine. 2.50.

Crotona. 550 B. C. Tripod, stork; rev., incused. Fine. 3.50.

Gela. 466 B. C. Man-headed bull; rev., horseman. Fine. 3.50.

Mytilene. Early type. Thick Didrachm. Two calves' heads butting; rev., punch mark. Fine. 6.00.

Metapontum. 550 B. C. Broad Didrachm. Ear of wheat; the same incused. Fine. 5.00.

Metapontum. Head of Mars; rev., ear of wheat. Almost uncirculated. 2.00.

Sybaris. 550 B. C. Broad Didrachm. Bull with head turned back; rev., same incused. Fine. 7.50.

Tarentum. 360 B. C. Naked horseman; rev., Taras on dolphin. Extremely fine. 2.50.

Thasos. 465 B. C. Satyr on knee bearing a nymph in his arms; rev., punch mark. Fine. 5.00.

Velia. 400 B. C. Head of Pallas; rev., lion devouring a skull. Fine. 2.50.

Egypt. Ptolemy VIII. 146 B. C. Didrachm. Head; rev., eagle. Fine. 2.00.

Drachms. Cnidus. Thick. Head of Venus in sunken square; rev., lion's head. Fine. 2.00.

Dyrrhachium. Cow suckling calf. Very fine. 2.00.

Massilia, Gaul. Head: rev., rude lion. Fine. 1.00.

Macedonia. Alexander the Great. B. C. 336. Very good. 1.25.

Spain. Head; rev., horseman. Very good. 1.00.

Sybaris. 530 B. C. Bull; rev., incused, Fine. 3.50.

Hemi-Drachms. Aegina. 700 B. C. Earliest period. Tortoise; rev., punch mark. Very good. 2.50.

Argos. 300 B. C. Wolf. Very fine. 1.00.

Cherosonesus. Forepart of lion. Fine. .75.

Caria. Lion's head and star. Very fine. 1.00.

Histiæa. Bacchante head; rev., female on prow. Extremely fine. 1.00.

Macedonia. Philip II. Head; rev., horseman. Very good. 1.00.

Messana. Hare. Fine. 1.00.

Miletas. Head; rev., lion. Fine. .50.

Phocis. Bull's head. Fine. 1.25.
Rhodes. An early type. Head; rev., flower in incused square. Very good. 1.00.
Sinope. Head; rev., harpy eagle. Good. .50.
Sicyon. Lion and dove. Fine. .75.
Thurium. Head; rev., bull. Very good. .75.
Persia. Darius I. 521 B. C. King as an archer. Rev., punch mark. Silver Daric. Very good. Rare. 5.00.
Sassanides. Broad Drachm. Size 21. Very fine. 1.50.
Sassanides. Small Drachm. Very fine. 1.00.

Peace Medals.

Libertas Americana. 1783. Beautiful head of Liberty with cap and pole; rev. Gallia protecting America from attacks of British lion. Size 30. Bronze proof. 3.50.
Libertas Americana. 1783. Louis XVI. on throne pointing to an American shield which a female is hanging on a pillar surmounted by a liberty cap; rev. Minerva holding shield. Tin. Very good. Size 29. Rare. 1.50.
Louis XVIII; rev., pedestal, America and France on either side; "Gallia et America fœderata, etc." Bronze proof. Size 32. 1.50.
1781. Netherlands. Four shields linked, "Gewapende Neutraliteit;" rev., "Jehovah," etc., in ten lines. Silver. Dull proof. 2.50.
Figure of Netherlands standing; "Netherland declares America free." Rev., a staff bearing flags of Holland and U. S., bales of goods and ship. "The Universal Wish, 1782." Silver proof. Size 22. 5.00.

Washington Medals.

Manly medal. Bust with aged features. "Geo. Washington, born Virginia Feb. 11, 1732." Rev., "General of American Armies 1775, resigned 1783, President of United States 1789." Original. Copper. Good. Size 31. 2.00.
Eccleston medal, Lancaster, 1805. Bust to right; rev., Indian with bow and arrow and "The land was ours" encircled by three lines of inscription. Bronze. Very fine, but lightly nicked. Size 48. 3.50.
Bust to left; George Washington, by F. B. Smith & Hartmann, N. Y.; rev., tomb of Washington; above, Fame flying. Bronze proof. Rare. Size 41. 5.00.
Bust to right, Paquet; rev., cabinet of Washington medals in U. S. Mint. Bronze. proof. Size 38. 1.25.
Bust. Paquet. Oath of Allegiance, br. pr., size 19. .35.
Bust, cherry tree scene, wood, size 36. .35.
Rare silver temperance token by Bale, size 12, pierced. 1.00.
Season medal. 1797. Man sowing grain. Bronze. Good. Rare. Size 29. 3.50.
Westwood medal. Bust to right; rev., "Made commander-in-chief," etc. Bronze. Size 26. 5.00.
Head to left. George Washington. Rev., "Born Feb. 22d, 1732," etc., in 6 lines. Silver proof. Weight 2 oz. Size 29. 3.00.
Liberty crowning bust of Washington on pedestal. Rev., Benevolence helping fallen man. 1808. Washington Benevolent Society, New York. Silver. Dull proof. Size 27. 2.00.
Washington. Rev., sword and fasces on altar. The Halliday medal. Very fine. Size 34. 2.50.
Bust; reverses, the different battles of 1776. Set of 8 pieces. Copper proofs. Size 22. 3.00.

Presidential Medals.

James Madison. Original silver peace medal. Bust to left; rev., clasped hands, pipe above. Pierced at top for suspension and has evidently been worn by the Indian who received it. Very fine and rare. Size 48. Weighs 5¼ oz. Av. 15.00.

Same. Bronze proof. Size 48. 1.50.
Same. Bust to right; rev., eagle, scroll, etc., w. m. proof. Size 40. 1.00.
James Monroe. Peace Medal. Bronze proof. Size 48. 1.50.
John Quincy Adams. Peace Medal. Br. proof. Size 48. 1.50.
Andrew Jackson. Peace Medal. Br. proof. Size 48. 1.50.
Same. Copper proof. Size 40. 1.00.
William H. Harrison. Bust to right; rev., battle of the Thames. Bronze proof. Size 42. 1.50.
Zachary Taylor. For Palo Alto. Bronze proof. Size 40. 1.50.
Same. Rev., scene of battle of Buena Vista. Bronze proof. Size 57. 3.00.
View of the Battle of Buena Vista; rev., pelican feeding young. Presented to Gen. Taylor by Louisiana. Bronze proof. Size 48. 3.00.
Zachary Taylor. Peace Medal. Bronze proof. Size 48. 1.50.
Millard Fillmore. Bust to right, 1850; rev., Pioneer and Indian before an American flag. Bronze proof. Size 40. 1.50.
James Buchanan. "Embassy from Japan." Bronze proof. Size 48. 1.50.
Same. "To Frederick Rose, Ass't Surgeon U. S. Navy." Group of figures. Bronze proof, slightly stained on edge. Size 48. 1.50.
Andrew Johnson. Rev., draped female with American flag grasping the hand of an Indian before a bust of Washington on a pedestal. Bronze proof. Size 48. 1.50.
Same as last, but *silver* proof. Weighs 6½ oz. Av. 10.00.
U. S. Grant. Bust, "The oceans united by railway, May 10, 1869;" rev., mountain scenery, train of cars, etc. Silver proof. Size 28. Morocco case. 3.00.

Miscellaneous American Medals.

John Egar Howard. For battle of Cowpens. Bronze proof. Size 29. 1.00.
Wm. Washington, same battle, bronze proof, size 29. 1.00.
"Light-horse Harry" Lee, for battle of Paulus Hook, N. J., 1779. Silver. Dull proof. Size 29. 3.50.
Col. Geo. Crogan. Defense of Fort Stephenson, 1813; rev., view of the battle. Bronze proof. Size 40. 1.50.
Gov. Isaac Shelby, for battle of Thames, 1813; rev., view of the battle. Bronze proof. Size 40. 1.50.
Maj.-Gen'l. Alexander Macomb; rev., view of battle of Plattsburgh. Bronze proof. Size 40. 1.50.
Maj.-Gen'l. Winfield Scott; rev., beautiful views of seven battles. Bronze proof. Size 56. 3.00.
Maj.-Gen'l. Winfield Scott; bust on square tablet, "The Commonwealth of Virginia," etc. Rev., column bearing names of battles in wreath. Bronze proof. Size 56. 3.00.
Maj.-Gen'l. Winfield Scott, for battle of Chippewa. Bronze proof. Size 40. 1.50.
Thos. Truxton; rev., scene of naval victory. Bronze proof. Size 36. 1.50.
Capt. James Biddle, capture of Penguin, 1815; rev., naval battle. Bronze proof. Size 40. 1.50.
Capt. Johnston Blakely, capture of Reindeer; rev., naval battle. Bronze proof. Size 40. 1.50.
John Paul Jones. For victories off Scottish coast; rev., naval scene. Bronze proof. Size 36. 1.00.
Franklin; by Dupre; rev., "Eripuit Cœlo," etc., in wreath. Bronze proof. Size 29. 1.25.
Franklin; rev., angel, br. proof, size 29. 1.25.
Franklin, bust in fur cap; rev., Franklin Institute, Pa. Bronze proof. Size 24. 1.00.
Lafayette, by Cannois; rev., "Appele parte volu unanime, etc." Silver. Dull proof. Size 32. Weight 2½ oz. Av. 5.00.
Lafayette, by Cannois; rev., "The defender," etc. Bronze proof. Size 30. 1.25.
Henry Clay; rev., hand on rock, inscribed "Constitution." Bronze proof. Size 48. 3.00.

Daniel Webster, by Wright; rev., column surmounted by a globe; "I still live" or
    base. " Liberty and Union, now and forever, one and inseparable.'
    Bronze proof. Size 48. In beautiful velvet-lined morocco case. 5.00.
Anthony Wayne. Copper proof. Size 22. .40.
Charles Carroll of Carrollton, by Gobrecht, on his 90th year; bronze proof; size 32
    3.00.
Wreck of Steamer Metis; rev., life-saving scene. Bronze proof. Size 40. 2.50.
Rescue of crew of U. S. Brig Somers, 1846; scene of wreck; rev., scene of rescue
    Bronze proof. Size 36. 2.00.
Humane Society of Massachusetts, 1866; shield with ship and boats, surmounted by
    house of refuge. Bronze proof. Size 36. 2.00.
Tayleur medal, " Fund for shipwrecked strangers," view of shipwreck. Bronze
    proof. Size 28. Rare. 2.00.
Sanitary Fair, Philadelphia, 1864, sick soldier, etc. Bronze proof. Size 36. 1.50.
Dr. Elisha Kane, bust above Arctic scene; rev., Masonic emblems. Bronze proof.
    Size 32. 1.25.
Edwin Forrest ; rev., date of birth. Bronze proof. Size 48. 3.50.
Agassiz, bust to right. Bronze proof. Size 29. 1.25.
Washington Irving ; rev,. date of birth. Bronze proof. Size 44. 3.50.
A. Thiers, from Philadelphia, 1873. Bronze proof. Size 29. 1.25.
Cyrus W. Field, for Atlantic Cable. Bronze proof. Size 32. 1.00.
Same. White metal proof. .25.
"Stonewall" Jackson, in japanned case, with glass to show each side. W. m. proof,
    size with case 56. .50.
Quinnipiack medal, minister preaching, 1638; rev., view of New Haven, etc. Very
    fine. Size 36. 2.00.
California State Agri. Soc. Award medal. Handsome landscape scene with ani-
    mals including a large bear, fruits, etc. Silver proof. Size 28. Weight
    1½ oz. Av. 2.50.
Hasty Pudding Club of Harvard College, 1795, making the pudding ; rev., sphinx.
    Octagon, size 26, silver proof, very rare. 3.50.
1849. Salem Charitable Mech. Assoc. Hercules has just killed a winged dragon ;
    boys picking apples from an impossible tree. Size 28. Bronze proof.
    1.25.
1860. Lake Erie. View of the engagement ; " We have met the enemy and they
    are ours," Lake Erie, Sep. 10th, 1813. Rev., " To Samuel Hatfield by res-
    olution of the Kentucky Legislature, Feb. 11, 1860." Gold. Proof. Unique.
    Weight, 666 grs. Size 26½. 75.00.

Centennial Medals.

The Centennial Award Medal, that granted to exhibitors. Seated female holding
    olive branch, four smaller designs and 38 stars surrounding ; rev , "Awarded
    by Centennial Commission." As these award medals are highly prized by
    the few who received them, scarcely any have been sold, and they are ex-
    tremely rare. Size 48. In velvet-lined morocco case. 10.00.
Centennial Commission Medal. Size 36. Brass proof. .50.
Same. Smaller, size 24. Silver proof. 1.25.
Same as last, brass proof in case. .40.
Independence Hall: legend, " Proclame Liberty, etc.;" rev., Memorial Hall, "To
    commemorate," etc. Bronze proof, size 37. in case. The handsomest U.
    S. Centennial Medal. 2.00.
French Centennial. Beautiful head of Liberty ; rev., crossed flags. Beautiful, ex-
    ceeds anything issued in U. S. Bronze proof. Size 32. 2.50.
Brazilian Centennial. Dom Pedro II. (The king that has been lately overthrown.)
    " Exposicao Internacional de Philadelphia, 1876." Very fine and rare.
    1.50.
Centennial. Wooden Medals. Oblong, 2½ x3 inches. Set of the five different
    buildings. 1.00.

Assay Medals.

1861. Head of Liberty. Br. proof. Size 21. 1.25.
1888. Grover Cleveland. Br. proof. Size 48. In handsome morocco velvet-lined
case. The largest of the Assay Medals. 5.00.
1889. Same as last, except date. In handsome velvet-lined wooden case. 5.00.

Foreign Medals.

(All bronze and perfect unless otherwise stated. Size given in sixteenths of an inch.)

Lord Byron, rev., poetic muse lamenting by the sea. 35. 2.50.
Flaxman, rev., Mercury carrying a muse. 36. 2.50.
Hogarth, rev., group of three male figures, 1848. 35. 2.50.
Wellington; rev., Vota Publica in wreath. 34. 1.50.
Wellington. 1815; rev., Minerva gives sword to Mars. 32. 2.00.
Lord Bacon, bust nearly facing; rev., Learning with starry robe flying over world.
Silver proof. 27. 4.00.
Louis XVI., bust to right; rev., large bust of Queen to left, by Duvivier 1781, a
beautiful medal. 47. 2.50.
Napoleon, rev., copy of star of legion of honor. Beautiful. 26. 2.00.
Napoleon, bust in cocked hat; rev., urn and sword, etc., funeral medal, 1840, by
Roget, very beautiful. 33. 2.50.
Napoleon; rev's., Fabius Cunctator, orphan of Legion of Honor, Egyptian eagle, the
Alps, etc. Silver proof or nearly proof. Size 25. Weight about 1½ oz.
Av. each. 7 pcs. Lot 20.00.
Louis Philippe; rev., France offering the crown, Aug. 9, 1830. Beautiful. 48.
3.50.
Louis Philippe, busts of king and queen in separate medallions facing; rev., medal-
lions with heads of the whole royal family surrounded with allegorical fig-
ures. A magnificent medal, exquisitely designed. 50. 3.50.
Napoleon III. Rev., Empress. By Montagny. 34. 2.00.
Rubens. Bust almost facing in large hat, an exquisite piece of workmanship by
Hart, 1840. Rev., his monument at Antwerp. Very rare. 46. 5.00.
Sandwich Islands. Award medal of Hawaian Society, beautiful obverse. 40.
2.00.
Poland. Magnificent bust of Augustus II. with draped armor and laurel wreath.
Rev., Hercules supporting the Polish world, both sides in extremely high
relief. A beautiful work of very light olive bronze. 45. 5.00.
Series of Roman Historical Tokens. Busts of Romulus, Numa Pompilius and other
distinguished rulers to Augustus, also of orators, poets, etc., views of land
and sea battles, etc., etc., all with explanatory inscriptions. No duplicates.
Very rare series published at Paris by J. Dassier & Son. Only set in
America. Silver. Size 20. Finest possible condition. 60 pcs. 50.00.
The magnificent Waterloo medal, with busts of the four Emperors. Exquisitely de-
signed. Filled electrotype shells. None issued in any other form. Size
88 (5½in.) 7.50.
Medallion plaques. Ebonized wood. 4⅜ inches in diameter, busts highly polished.
Queen Victoria and Prince Albert; Albert Edward, Prince of Wales, and
Alexandra, Princess; Napoleon III. and Eugenie; Napoleon I. and Victor
Emmanuel II. 8 pcs. Lot for 5.00.
Wagner. Fine portrait by Wiener. Rev., characters representing his different
operas grouped on bridge inscribed BAYREUTH. Beautifully designed and
executed. Bronze proof. Size 45. 5.00.
England. Geo. III. Bust to left, 1801; rev., two females joining hands. Com-
memorating union of England and Ireland. Bronze proof. Size 51. Very
rare. 2.50.
England. William IV. 1830. A superb frosted silver medal by Chantry, surrounded by producing silver land to perfect medal. Also weight. etc.
" Adelaide regina coll. gust. 1830. " wreath, etc. Extremely
fine. Excessively rare. Weight 5 ... Size 44. 2.50.

Masonic Medals.

Hopkins Lodge, Black Jack Grove, Texas. Silver, brass and copper proofs. Size 14. Lot 1.00.

Maryland Commandery, No. 1. 1790–1871. Brass, silver plated. Triangular Size 36. Marvin 25. 1.25.

Mary Commandery, No. 36, Phil'a. Christ and Mary. Bronze, shield-shaped, per fect. Size 23x30. 1.50.

Lake City Lodge, Florida, No. 27. Marvin 290. Brass proof. Size 18. .35.

St. Albans, Phil'a, No. 47. Shield shaped Centennial. Tin. Size 24x32. .25.

Solomon's Lodge, No. 1. Po'keepsie, N. Y. Head of Washington. Copper and brass proofs. Size 22. Pair. 75.

"Hollandsche Loge Staat Van Nieuw York, 5787." Copper proof. Size 20. .50.

Official Badge, Triennial Conclave, San Francisco, 1883, Masonic Cross with Arms of California pendant from a bear. Cross, size 24; bear, size 20. 2.50.

Triennial Conclave, San Francisco. Knight on horseback. Gold. Size 8. 1.00.

Phil'a Commandery's Pilgrimage to San Francisco. Brass proof. Size 20. Marvin 84. .35.

Triennial Conclave, Chicago, 1880. Masonic Cross (size 24) with pin and ribbon Tin. 1.00.

Grand Lodge of Canada, 1858. Marvin 40. Tin. Size 26. Very fine. .75.

"Lodge de la Parfaite Egalite O'de Rouen" Skeletons and Masonic emblems Silver. Fine. Size 20. 2.50.

"Du Point Parfait A L'o—De Paris." Marvin 164. Bronze. About proof. Size 18. .75.

" Les Pyramids O—D' Alexandrie Egypte." Sphinx, obelisk, etc.; pyramids in background, all-seeing eye above. Bronze proof. Size 29. Marvin 49 2.50.

Egyptain Obelisk. Marvin 712. Silver proof. Size 22. 1.50.

Same. Bronze proof. .75

Head of Minerva with Pegasus and owl on crested helmet, 5776–5876. Centennial Homage from European Brethren to American Masons. Bronze. Size 24. A beauty. 1.50.

Philadelphia Commandery, No. 2. Bell-shaped Centennial. Silvered. Perfect Size 32x32. .50.

Olive Branch, No. 39, N. Y. W. metal proof. Size 26. .25.

Kadosh Commandery, No. 23, Phila. W. metal, proof, size 29. .35.

Badge of 18th Degree, Royal Scotch. Double headed eagle at top (size 16x18), pin attached ; ribbon, pendant from which a crowned compass inclosing a stork feeding her young, cross above (size 24x36) Total length 4 inches. 3.50.

Miscellaneous Cards, etc.

1822 Dime counterstamped with heads of Lafayette and Washington in procession, 1824 (reception of Lafayette). 2.50.

1820 Cent, similar counterstamp, the best impression of these counterstamps I have seen. 2.50.

Beck's Public Baths. Female washing her feet. Rare card. Very good. 1.50.

1837. Card of Nathan C. Folger, New Orleans. Brass. Size 22. Very fine. One in the Levick sale bought $11.25. 3.50.

10 cents. Encased postage stamp. 2.00.

5 cents. Encased postage stamp. Bailey & Co., Phil'a. 1.50.

3 cents. Encased postage stamp. Drake's Bitters. 1.25.

Am I not a Woman and a Sister ? Negress in chains. Very fine. .50.

Am I not a Man and a Brother? Negro in chains. Very fine. Rare. 1.50.

Same obverse but larger. Size 21. Tin. Good. 1.00.

Same design, cameo, negro in black. Oval. Size 17x20. Very fine. 2.00.

Washington. "Carry me to Atwood's Railroad Hotel. 243 Bowery, and my face is good for 3 cents." Rare early card. Good. 1.00.

Lee and Reynolds, Cheyenne Agency. Nickle card. **Size 20.** Buffalo on obverse. Fine and rare. 1.00.

First Steam Coinage at U. S. Mint, Mar. 23, 1836. Cap in rays. Bronze proof. Size 18. .25.

Same but dated Feb 22, 1836. Very good. Rare. .50.

John Brown, "Slavery the sum of all villainies;" rev., Brown hanging. 1859. W. m. proof. Size 20. 1.00.

"No submission to the North," 1860. Palmetto tree, cannon, etc. Rev., "The Wealth of the South," rice, tobacco, sugar, cotton. Copper, brass and tin. Also, reverse muled with shield, tin and brass, and with John Bell in copper. 6 pieces. Perfect. Rare lot. 3.00.

Jeff Davis hanging; rev., "Death to traitors." Brass token. Uncirculated. 1.00.

Swedish Plate Money.

Two Dalers. Frederick. Counterstamped F. R. S. 1743 crowned in each corner. 2 DALER SILF MYNT in centre. Very fine. Measures 7x7¾ inches. 12.50.

One Daler. 1745. Same design. Very fine. 7.50.

Copper Coins and Medals of British America.

1759, Geo. II. Bust to left; rev., victories at Quebec, Crown Point, etc. Bronze. Very fine. Size 27. 2.50.

1674. Bust of Louis XIV., in flowing hair. Rev., emblematic of victory over the Dutch at Martinque. Bronze proof. Size 26. 2.50.

1690. Same obverse. Rev., France seated on trophy, beaver at her feet, river-god to right. KEBECA LIBERATA. Bronze proof. Size 26. 3.00.

1886. Brantford, Ont., Thayendanagea : fine bust of the chief; rev., his monument. Bronze proof. Size 24. 1.50.

Halifax Ferry Token. Steamboat. Uncirculated. Bright red, nearly proof. 2.00.

White's Farthing, Halifax. Very fine. 5.00.

1838. Side-view Halfpenny. "Bank of Montreal" on reverse label. Fine. Extremely rare. 20.00.

1839. Side view Halfpenny. Fine. Extremely rare. 12.50.

Starr and Shannon. Indian and dog. Extremely fine. Light olive. .75.

Francis Mullins & Son. Very fine. 1.00.

Robert Purvis. Uncirculated. .75.

H. Gagnon. Beaver. Uncirculated. 1.25.

T. S. Brown & Co. Fine. Brown. .35.

J. Shaw & Co. Fine. Brown. .35.

J. Brown. Fine. Brown. .35.

Carriett & Alport. Fine. Brown. .50.

Miles W. White. Fine. Brown. .50.

W. A. & S. Black. Fine. .50.

John Alexander. Fine. .35.

Hostermann & Etter. 1814. Fine. .50.

Same. 1815. Smaller. Fine. .35.

Lesslie & Sons. Half-penny. Fine. .25.

Ship, "Halifax" below. Fine. .35.

"No labour, no bread." Very fine. .35.

Rutherford Brothers, Newfoundland. Very choice. .25.

Magdalen Island. Seal and dried codfish. Fine. 1.50.

Montreal and Lachine Railroad Co. Engine and beaver. Large. Extra fine. 3.00.

Montreal. "De l'isle de Montreal a Repentigny on Lachesnaye." "Charette" token. Fine. Very rare. 10.00.

Nova Scotia and New Brunswick. Ship, "Success" below. About uncirculated. Light olive. 5.00.

Ships, Colonies and Commerce. Rev., harp. As usually found. Unknown to Le-
Roux. 5.00.
Canada. A large collection, good to very fine. Le Roux Nos. 7, 12, 18, 21, 25,
27, 28, 29, 32, 33, 34, 38, 39, 40, 41, 42, 43, 45, 50, 51, 55, 71, 78, 80, 83,
91, 93, 95, 96, 97, 99, 101, 104, 118, 119, 127, 129, 143, 144, 160, 165, 166,
167, 171, 176, 179, 180, 181, 187, 188, 190, 191, 196, 197, 200, 202, 203,
206, 210, 211, 214, 216, 217, 218, 220, 223, 226, 227. 68 pcs. Lot for 6.00.

Continental and Colonial Notes, Badges, Etc.

Continental. 1775; May 10, $3. 1776, May 9, $2, 4. July 22, $3, 30. Nov. 2,
$4, 8. 1777, Feb. 26, $4, 8. May 20, $30. 10 pieces. Fine lot. 2.50.
1776. $⅙, ⅓, ½, ⅔. Sun dial. "Mind your business." Fine. Lot 1.00.
1778. April 11. $4. Yorktown. Very fine. 5.00.
1778. April 11. $5. Yorktown. Fine. 5.00.
1778. April 11. $6. Yorktown. Fine. 5.00.
1778. April 11. $7. Yorktown. Very fine. 5.00.
1778. April 11. $30. Yorktown. Very fine. 5.00.
Vermont. 1781. Feb., 2s. 6d. Fine and excessively rare. 35.00.
Massachusetts. Jan. 22, 1777. £10. An extremely large and very rare note.
6¾x7¾ inches. Very fine. Signed by W. Cooper and N. Appleton.
7.50.
Delaware. 1758. May. 1. 20sh. Printed by Ben Franklin. Lion on reverse.
Very good. 1.00.
North Carolina. 1776. April 2, $10. Peacock. Good. .75.
1778. $5, 10, 20. Good. Lot. 1.50.
Georgia. 1777. Oct. 16. 1sh, 2sh. 6d, 5, 10, 20sh. Long notes. Hand hold-
ing Constitution. Uncirculated. Lot. 12.50.
1778. $30. Blue hog. Very fine. 5.00.
1778. $40. Hand holding dagger and dove. Very fine. 5.00.
Hungarian Independence. Louis Kossuth. Feb. 2, 1852. $1. Uncirculated. 1.00.
Badges. Harrison. Campaign of 1840. Portrait of Harrison, typical figures,
eagle, owl and beaver above, "Tippecanoe and Fort Meigs" below. 1.50.
Henry Clay. Portrait. Indian with shield above. .50.
Lafayette. Old, 1824 probably. 1.00.
Washington. Centennial Celebration, 1832. .50.
American Manufactures and Ireland's Independence Solidarity with attached medal,
size 24, "We purpose 'fore high heaven till Erin's chains are riven," etc.
.50.

Fractional Currency.

(All new and clean.)

5, 10 Cents. Perforated edges. 2.50.
50, 25, 10, 5 Cents. Plain edges. 2.00.
50, 25, 10, 5 Cents. Washington in gilt ring. 2.50.
50, 25, 10, 5 Cents. Washington in gilt ring. Paper that will split. 5.00.
50 Cents. Justice. Red back. Auto. sign. of Colby and Spinner. Coarse fibre
paper. 5.00.
50 Cents. Justice. Red back. No letters on rev. 2.50.
50 Cents. Justice. Green back. Coarse fibre paper. 3.50.
50 Cents. Justice. Green back. 2.00.
50 Cents. Spinner. Red back. 2.25.
50 Cents. Spinner. Green back. "50" at ends. 1.50.
50 Cents. Spinner. Green back. "50" in centre. 1.75.
25 Cents. Fessenden. Red back. 1.50. Green back. .50.
25 Cents. Fessenden. Green back. Coarse fiber paper, gilt letters on reverse.
Heavy but not solid disc. 5.00.
25 Cents. Fessenden. Green back. Coarse fiber paper. Solid discs. 20.00.
15 Cents. Grant and Sherman. Red back. Auto. sign. of Allison and Spinner. 8.00.

10 Cents. Washington. Red back. Auto. sign. of Colby and Spinner. 1.50.
10 Cents. Washington. Red back. 1.00. Green back. .35.
5 Cents. Clark. Red back. .75. Green back. .35.
3 Cents. Washington. .40. Dark curtain. .75.
50 Cents. Lincoln. 1.50.
50 Cents. Stanton. .85.
25 Cents. Washington. .50.
15 Cents. Liberty. .60.
10 Cents. Liberty. .35.
50 Cents. Dexter. .75.
25 Cents. Walker. .50.
10 Cents. Merideth. Green seal. .50. Red seal. .25.
Shield of Fractional Currency as issued by U. S. Contains two Grant and Sherman
    15 cent notes, etc. Framed. For shipment, no glass. 15.00.

The following are all signed in autograph on the reverse.

50 Cents. Crawford. Auto. sign. of " Jno. C. New." 5.00.
50 Cents. Crawford. Auto. sign. of " B. K. Bruce, Register U. S. Treasury."
    5.00.
50 Cents. Crawford. Auto. sign. of " Jas. Gilfillan, Treasurer U. S." 5.00.
50 Cents. Crawford. Auto. sign. of " A. U. Wyman, Treasurer U. S." 5.00.
25 Cents. Walker. Auto. sign. of " B. K. Bruce, Register U. S. Treasury." 5.00.
25 Cents. Walker. Auto. sign. of " Jas. Gilfillan, Treasurer U. S." 5.00.
25 Cents. Walker. Auto. sign. of " A. U. Wyman, Treasurer U. S." 5.00.
10 Cents. Merideth. Auto. sign. of " Jas. Gilfillan, Treasurer U. S." 5.00.
10 Cents. Merideth. Auto. sign. of " A. U. Wyman, Treasurer U. S." 5.00.
5 Cents. Clark. Red and green backs. Both with auto. sign. of Clark on reverse.
    Pair 10.00.

The following are all extremely rare.

50 Cents. 2nd issue. No gilt ring around Washington. Coarse fiber paper. Plain
    reverse. 7.50.
50 Cents. 2nd issue. The obverse has the large gilt outline 50 and gilt figures in
    corners usually found on the reverse, otherwise plain. The reverse is the
    usual design, but with the gilt ring usually found on the obverse around the
    50, and lacking the designs which on this note are on the obverse. Coarse
    fiber paper. 7.50.
50 Cents. 2nd issue. Obverse plain except a gilt ring; reverse as usual. Coarse
    fiber paper. 7.50.
10 Cents. 2nd issue. Obverse plain except a gilt ring; reverse as usual. Coarse
    fiber paper. 7.50.
5 Cents. 2nd issue. Obverse plain; reverse lacks the outlined figure and is differ-
    ently shaded from the regular note, the eagle and stars on border being light
    where dark on the usual note and vice versa. The color is a light gold-
    brown. Unique. 15.00.

Hard Times Tokens.

Negress in chains. " Am I not a woman and a sister?" Very good. .25.
Steer. " A friend to the Constitution." Rev., ship, " Agriculture and Commerce."
    Very good. .75.
Donkey. Rev., turtle, Uncirculated. Bright red. .25.
Loco Foco. Uncirculated. Bright and olive. One of best I have seen. 1.25.
Head of Jackson; rev., hog running. Uncirculated. Partly bright. .40.
Same. Brass. Uncirculated. 2.00.
Jackson in safe; rev., ship. Uncirculated. Beautiful purple color. .75.
Ship; rev., wrecked ship. Uncirculated. Purple and bright. .40.
1837. Liberty head. 13 stars. No. 27. Very good. 1.00.
1837. Liberty head. 15 stars (a small star on each side of date). No. 28. Very
    good. 1.00.
1837. " United " head, large date. No. 29. Good. 1.00.

Ancient and **Foreign Gold.**

Ancient Scythian gold coin, Ardokro. King at fire altar; rev., king seated on throne. Extremely fine and very rare. Size 14. 15.00.

Turkey. Gold. Proof. Size 14. 2.00.

Transylvania. 1657. George Rakoczi II. Ducat. Uncirculated. 6.00.

Russia. 1833. *Beautiful Proof Set of the Platinum Coinage.* 3, 6, 12 Roubles. A splendid and rare set. 50.00.

Salzburg. 1714. Francis Anton. ¼ Ducat. Uncirculated. 2.00.

Nordlingen. 1497. Ducat. The 4 in loop form. One of the earliest dated coins. Very fine. 7.50.

Austria. 1643. Ferdinand III. 5 Ducats. Brilliant mint lustre. A beauty. 20.00.

Nurnberg. Two pretty little gold coins with lamb and standard. The smallest is only 7 cts. in gold. Uncirculated. Pair 3.00.

England. 1794. George III. Spade Guinea. Uncirculated. Proof surface. 7.50.

England. 1817. George III. Sovereign. St. George and dragon. Uncirculated or barely touched. 6.50.

Japan. Yen or Dollar. Uncirculated. 1.75.

Guatemala. 1860. Peso or Dollar. Uncirculated. 1.75.

Guatemala. 1860. 4 Reals. Uncirculated. 1.25.

Costa Rica. 1850. Dollar. Undraped female leaning on column. About uncirculated. 2.00.

Costa Rica. 1866. Peso. Very good. 1.50.

New Grenada. 1837. Dollar. About uncirculated. 1.75.

Honduras. 1846. Dollar. Mountain peaks. Uncirculated. 1.75.

Mexico. 1826-1828-1862. Dollars. About uncirculated. Lot 5.00.

Spain. 1757-1760-1762-1777-1786-1788. Dollars. About uncirculated. Lot 10.00.

Roman. (457) Leo I. Rev., Victory holding a cross. Solidus. Very good. 5.00.

(474) Zeno. Rev., Victory holding a cross. Solidus. Very good. 5.00.

(630) Heraclius and son. Rev., cross on pedestal. Solidus. Very fine. 6.00.

Oriental Silver.

Anam. Taele or Dragon Dollar. Grinning human-faced dragon's head above sun; rev., 4 characters around sun. Uncirculated. Rare. 5.00.

Anam. Silver duk. Dragons. Extremely fine. 2.00.

Oudh, India. Wadschid Ali. 1850. ⅛ rupee. Two mermaids. Very fine. 1.50.

Bidsnagur, India. Half Fanam. Dancing deity. Very fine. 1.00.

Madras. Quarter Pagoda. Tower surrounded by stars; rev., god Vishnu in circle of dots. Fine. 1.50.

Assam. Octagonal Rupee. Very fine. Rare. 2.00.

Burmah. Rupee, ½, ¼ and ⅛. Peacock with spread tail. Very fine. Set for 5.00.

Japan. Itzebue. Uncirculated. .75.

Japan. ¼ Itzebue. Uncirculated. .35.

Siam. Bullet money. Tical. Very fine. 1.25.

Siam. Bullet money. ¼ and ⅛ Tical. Very fine. Each .75.

Persia. ¼ Kran. Sun-lion with sword (dime size). Uncirculated. .50.

Japan. Oblong silver coin, 3½x1⅜ in. The obverse is covered with characters, also two circular stamps with characters near each end. Fine and rare. Weight 4½ oz. Av. 10.00.

Japan. Oblong, one pear shaped, silver dumps, each stamped with characters. They range in size from a pea to ¾ oz. I do not think two sizes are alike. Fine lot. 13 pieces. 12.50.

Siam. Circulars coin with elephant and royal umbrellas. 2, 1, ½, ¼, ⅛ Tical. Uncirculated. 6.00.

Corea. 1 and 2 Stubs (size 14 and 18.) Coined as indemnity money to China. Obverse with porcelain centre; rev., four characters. Very curious and rare. Uncirculated. Pair for 5.00.

Siam. Bullet money. 4, 2, 1, ½, ¼, ⅛, ½ Tical Full set except ⅟₁₆ Tical. Fine and desirable. 10.00.

Anam. Loaf shaped, or more properly something like a cap with two visors. Bears three counter-stamps, two of which are from dies, one native characters—the other English, and the third being the autograph of some native merchant. Remarkable as to weight, which is 12 oz. Av. Fine and desirable. 25.00.

Anam. Coin similar to last, but outside and edges smoothly polished, die stamp on bottom, and four characters on top. 5.00.

Cambodia. Silver coins. Obverses, odd bird and bird idol. Very fine. Size 8 Each, .50.

Saurashtran, Hindu. Curious figure somewhat resembling a pelican. Size 10 Fine. 1.50.

India. Small dump with idol. Fine. .50.

Morocco. 1284. Size 12. Very good. .40.

Zanzibar. 1299. Size 10. Uncirculated. Rare. .75.

Foreign Silver.

New Grenada. 1849. Head of Liberty. Pattern Peso by Wyon. 4 designs. *Beautiful proofs.* Lot for 10.00.

Sweden. 1871. Chas. XV. 4 R. M., 2 R. M., 50, 25, 10 Ore. *Beautiful proofs.* Set for 5.00.

Central America. Dollar. Sun rising behind mountain peaks. But little circulated. Semi-proof. 1.50.

Republic of Columbia. Indian head and pomegranate. 2, 8 Reals. Very good. Pair. 1.75.

U. S. of Colombia. 1868. Half Dollar. Very fine. 1.00.

Bolivia. 1845. Llamas under tree. Dollar. Uncirculated. Mint lustre. 2.50.

Peru. 1833. Liberty standing. Dollar. Barely circulated. Mint lustre. 2.00.

Peru. 1862, 1863, 1864. Callao and Lima. Indian, Liberty in chariot, steamboat. Tokens. ¼ dollar size. Semi-proof. 3 pieces. Lot. 2.50.

Chili. 1874. Dollar. Condor. Barely circulated. 1.50.

Chili. Mining Dollar. Plain planchet with star and 1 P. in sunken counterstamp. Fine. 2.00.

La Plata. 1, 2, 4, 8 Reals (Dollar). Sun in Rays. Very fine. Lot. 3.00.

Cordoba. (Argentine Conf.) Dollar. Fort surrounded by seven flags. Very fine· Rare. 5.00.

Uruguay. 1877. 50, 20, 10 Centavos. Mint lustre. Lot for 1.25.

Venezuela. 1858. Half Dollar. Fine. 1.00.

Ecuador. 1855. Half Dollar. Fine. 1.00.

Caracas. 1811. 2 Reals. Very fine. Rude. .40.

France. Louis XIIII. 1653. Crown. Young head. Very fine. 2.50.

Bavaria. Maximilian II. 1853. ½, 1, 2 Gulden. 1 Thaler. Uncirculated. Mint bloom. Lot 2.50.

Papal States. Pius IX. 1869. ½, 1, 2 Lire. Proof surface. Lot 1.15.

Spain. Ferd. VI. 1755. Mexico mint. Dollar. Crowned globes between pillars. A splendid specimen in nearly brilliant proof condition. 4.00.

Neapolitan Republic. Liberty standing. Year 7. Fine. 2.50.

Russia. 1860. Rouble. Proof. 1.00.

Sicily. 1855. Ferd. II. Crown. Uncirculated. 1.25.

Straits Settlements. 10 Cents. Extremely fine. .25.

Sandwich Islands. Kalakaua I. Dime. Brilliant proof. .50.

Japan. Dragon. Yen, 50, 20, 10, 5 sen. Uncirculated. Lot 2.50.

Ceylon. 1821. Elephant. Rix dollar. Uncirculated. 2.00.

Bolivia. 1868. Pattern set. 5, 10, 20 Centavos, 1 Boliviano. State Arms. Rev. Condor standing. Silver proofs. 7.50.

Bolivia. 1884. 5, 10, 20, 50 Centavos, 1 Boliviano. State Arms. Brilliant proofs. 7.50.

Sierra Leone. 1791. Dollar. Lion. Fine. 2.50.

Ecuador. Sucre (Dollar) and ½ Sucre. Uncirculated. Mint lustre. Pair 2.00.

Sandwich Islands. 1883. Kalakaua I. Dollars, ½, ¼, 1/10. Uncirculated. Mint lustre. Set 3.50.

Hayti. 1881. Gourde (Dollar), 20, 10 cts. Beautiful design. Brilliant mint lustre. Set 2.50.

China. Mexican Dollar with Chinese chop-mark. 1.25.

Switzerland. 1814. Canton Soloth'n. Crown. Fine. 2.00.

New Grenada. 1847. 2, 8 Reals. Very fine. Scarce. Pair 1.50.

Bolivia. 1884. Dime. Br. Proof. .50.

Sardinia. 1859. Victor Emmanuel. 5 Lire. Brilliant mint lustre. 1.50.

Papal States. 1836. Gregory XVI. Scudo. Uncir'd. 1.50.

Austria. 1780. Maria Theresa. Levant Crown. Uncir'd. 1.50.

Brunswick. 1670, etc. Wild man. 4, 6, 12, 24 Gros. Very fine. Lot 2.50.

Mexico. 1866. Maxmilian. Dollar and half. Barely circulated. Pair 2.50.

1841. Bolivia. Bolivar. Llamas under tree. Dollar. Barely cir'd. 1.50.

1837. South Peru. Dollar. Human-faced sun: rev., volcano, ship, fort, etc. Barely circulated. 1.50.

1842. Peru. Dollar. Liberty with spear and shield. Very fine. Mint lustre. 1.50.

1867. Peru. Dollar. Seated Liberty. Uncirculated. 1.25.

1877. Chili. Dollar. Condor. Uncirculated. 1.50.

Japan. Dollar. Dragon and sun. Uncirculated. 1.50.

Japan. 50 Sen. Dragon. Uncirculated. .75.

1821. Spain. Ferd. VII. Dollar. About uncirculated. 1.25.

1817. Spain. Ferd. VII. Dollar. Counterstamped for Brazil. Extremely fine. 1.25.

Tranquebar. Dump with idol. Very fine. .65.

France. Napoleon III. 1852. ½, 1 fr. Uncirculated. 2 pcs. Lot. .50.

Mexico. 1808. Aug. 15. Arms crowned. Proclamation medal. Size 18. Extremely fine. 1.25.

Mexico. 1821. Oct. 27. Secretary bird on cactus. Proclamation of Independence medal. Br. proof. Size 22. 1.50.

Mexico. 1822. July 21. Same design. Inauguration medal of Augustin. Size 22. Barely touched proof. 1.25.

Another. All but as fine. 1.00.

San Luis Potosi. Indian queen seated. Medal for its patriots. Size 19. About uncirculated. 1.50.

India. Old rupee, curious die counterstamp of man on horseback. Very fine. 2.00.

Assam. Octagonal rupee, curious dragon at bottom, extremely fine. 2.00.

Assam. Octagonal ¼, ½, 1 rupee, very fine. 3 pcs. Lot. 3.00.

Triangular sections of Spanish coins, three counter-stamped with C (Cayenne ?), one with 3. Fine. 4 pcs. Lot. 3.50.

SILVER COINS OF GREAT BRITAIN. 47

Kempten. Bust of the Bishop. Bracteates. Size 14. Uncirculated. 10 pcs. Lot. 2.50.
Lille. Marshal's batons crowned, rev., mailed arm with sword. "Non sine numine," necessity money, very fine, size 19. 1.50.
France. Louis XV. 1721. Bust with long curls. View of islands, "Guadalupa insula muneta. Philippo regente." Brilliant proof. Size 26. 2.50.
Scene of Manger, odd design, very fine. Size 22. 1.00.
Turkey. Cup-shaped coins. Size 23 (2), 18. Fine but pierced. 3 pcs. Lot. 1.00.
Venice. 1734, etc. Kneeling saints, winged lion. Largest (size 20), fine, other (size 13) good, one pierced. 2 pcs. Pair. 1.00.
Small bracteates. 25 pcs. Lot. 1.00.
Zacatecas. 1811. Provisional dollar. Very fair. 2.00.
Zacatecas. Ferd. VII. Provisional 2 reals. Very fair. .50.
Zacatecas. Mountain with cross. 2 reals. Very fair. .75.
Mexico. 1812. Vargas dollar. Fair (never found better). 1.25.
Central America. Sun rising behind mountain peaks. 1, 2 reals. Pair. .50.
Guatemala. 1760. Chas. III. Proclamation 2 reals. Good, but twice pierced. Rare. .40.
Guatemala. 1808. Ferd. VII. Proclamation 2 reals. Mountain. Very good. 1.50.
Same. 1 real. Good. Pierced. .35.
Guatemala. Sept. 24, 1812. 2 reals. Open book in rays, arms of Guatemala. Fine. Pierced. .50.
Louis XV. and XVI. Tokens. 1735, 1741, etc. ½, ¼ (3) Crowns. Ship under full sail, Justice with scales, tree growing, etc. Fine. 4 pcs. 2.50.
Republic. 1849. 20, 50c., 1, 5 Francs. Uncirculated. Mint bloom. Lot. 1.75.
Republic. 1852. Louis Napoleon Bonaparte. 50c., 1, 5 Francs. Uncirculated. Mint bloom. 1.75.
Chili. 1817. Dollar. Volcano; rev., pillar surmounted by globe. Barely circulated. Lustre. 2.00.
Prussia. 1871. Siege Thaler. Fine. 1.00.
Spain. Dollar counterstamped with head of Geo. III. of England to pass current in that country. Fine. 2.50.
Berne. 1795. Dollar. Swiss soldier. Rev., Bear on shield. Proof. A beauty. 5.00.
Canton Zurich. 1813. Dollar. Semi-proof. A beauty. 5.00.
Canton Appenzell. 1816. Dollar. Swiss soldier. Rev., dancing bear. Semi-proof. A beauty. 5.00.
Canton Luzerne. 1814. Dollar. Swiss soldier. Proof. A beauty. 5.00.
Persia. Sun-lion with sword. 2 Francs. Uncirculated. 1.00.
Chili. 1839. Dollar. Condor breaking chains. Barely circulated. 1.50.
Peru. 1822. Dollar. Coat of arms with flags; rev., Justice and Liberty standing beside column. Fine and rare. 2.00.
France. 1844. Louis Philippe. 5 Francs. Br. proof. 2.50.
1789. Louis XVI. Crown. About uncirculated. 3.00.
1792. Louis XVI. Crown. Bust. Rev., angel inscribing tablet, cock and fasces on sides. Fine. 1.75.

Silver Coins of Great Britain.

Early British. Cunobeline. Head to right. Rev., Pegasus on dotted base. Gold ¼ Stater. Extremely fine. 7.50.
Early British Tetradrachm. Idiotic head; rev., shadowy horseman on colossal horse. Very fine. 6.00.
Stycae. Rude horse. Copper. Fine. 1.50.
Ethelred II. 978. Head fileted. Rev., small cross in circle. Silver penny. Extremely fine. 3.00.

Ethelred II. 978. Holding sceptre, large cross on rev. Silver penny. Very
    fine. 2.00.
Edward the Confessor. 1042. Silver penny. Bust with sceptre. SWETHAM
    ON LYN. Extremely fine. 3.00.
Another. Larger bust. Extremely fine. 3.00.
Another. King enthroned. Chichester mint. Very fine. 3.00.
William the Conqueror. 1066. Silver penny. Fine. 2.00. Good. 1.50.
Henry II. 1154. Silver penny. Good. 1.00.
Henry III. 1216. Silver penny. Very good. .50.
Edward I. 1272. Silver penny. Fine. .50.
Edward I. 1272. Groat. Good. .75.
Edward II. 1307. Silver penny. Fine. .50.
Edward III. 1327. Half Groat. Fine. .75.
Henry IV. 1399. Groat. Fine. .75.
Henry VI. 1422. Groat. Very fine. 1.00.
Henry VI. 1422. Silver penny. Very fine. .75.
Henry VII. 1485. Half Groat. Very good. Rare. 1.00.
Henry VIII. 1509. Groat. Side view. Fine. .75.
Henry VIII. 1509. Groat. Front face. Fine. 1.00. Good. .50.
Henry VIII. 1509. Silver penny. Very fine. .75. Very fair. .40.
Edward VI. 1547. Broad Shilling. Very fine. 2.00. Fine. 1.50.
Mary. 1553. Groat. Very fine. 2.00. Good. 1.25.
Mary. 1553. Groat. Bust of Mary. Legend "Philip and Maria." Fine. 2.00.
Elizabeth. 1601. Crown. Very good, fine for this piece. Very rare. 20.00.
Elizabeth. 1558. Shilling. Fine. .75.
Elizabeth. 1561. Sixpence. Fine. .60. Good. .35.
Elizabeth. 1562. Milled Sixpence. Extremely fine. 2.00.
James I. 1603. Half Crown. King on horseback. Very fair. 1.25.
James I. 1603. Shilling. Fine. 1.25. Very good. .75.
James I. 1603. Sixpence. Extremely fine. 1.25. Fine. .75. Good. .50.
Charles I. 1625. Half Crown. King on horseback. Good. 2.00.
Charles I. 1625. Shilling. Fine. .75. Good. .50.
Charles I. 1625. Oromond Crown, Half Crown, Shilling and Sixpence. Good.
    Set for 20.00.
Commonwealth. 1653. Twopence. Fine. 1.00.
Commonwealth. 1653. Penny. Fine. 1.00. Good. .75.
Commonwealth. 1653. Halfpenny. Fine. Rare. 1.50.
Oliver Cromwell. 1658. Crown. A beautiful uncirculated specimen, the crack in
    the die scarcely showing. 50.00.
Oliver Cromwell. 1658. Crown. Only the barest touch of circulation on most
    prominent parts of obverse. 30.00. Another, fine. 20.00.
Oliver Cromwell. 1658. Half Crown. Extremely fine. 20.00. Very good. 10.00.
Oliver Cromwell. 1658. Shilling. Barely circulated. 15.00. Fine. 10.00.
Charles II. 1665. Pattern farthing in silver. Uncirculated. 3.50.
William and Mary. 1693. Half Crown. Rev., 4 shields, monogram W M and
    date in angles. Very good. 1.50.
William III. 1697. Half Crown. Good. 1.00.
Anne. 1707. Crown. Rev., roses and plumes in the angles. Fine. 3.00.
1804. Bank of England. Dollar. Fine. 1.75.
Geo. III. 1818, 1819. Pistrucci Crown. St. George and the dragon. Proof. 7.50.
Scotland. David II. 1329. Silver Penny. Crowned bust. Very fine. 2.00.
Robert II. 1370. Groat. Very good. 1.50.
Mary. Billion Plack. Thistle. Good. 1.50.
Mary. "Nonsunt." M. crowned. Rev., "I AM NON SVNT DVO SED VNA
    CARO." Good. 2.00.
James VI. 1594. Thistle Mark. Bust of James; rev., thistle. Fine. 5.00.
James VI. 1601. Thistle Mark. Shield; rev., thistle. Fine. 5.00.
Ireland. 1723. **Wood** Sixpence. Similar in design to the Wood halfpence, which

were rejected in Ireland and then extensively circulated in America. Extremely fine and *excessively rare*. 25.00.

James I. Shilling. Bust; rev., harp. "Henricus Rosas Regna Jacobus." Very good. 2.00.

Foreign Coppers.

Where more than one piece is given on a line, the price is for all and not per piece.

Antigua. 1836. Palm tree. Farthing. Fine. .50.

Argentine Confederation. Head of Liberty. 1, 2 Centavos. Uncirculated. Bright red. .50.

Andora. 1873. 10 Centimes. Proof. The only coin of this little republic. .25.

Bolivia. 1883. 1, 2 Centavos. Proof. .50.

British Honduras. 1885. Cent. Uncirculated. Bright red. .25.

Barbadoes. Penny. Negro head and pineapple. Fine. .75. Good. .50.

Barbadoes. Penny and Halfpenny. Neptune in car. Also, Penny. Pineapple. Set of 3 pcs. Proofs. Handsome. 15.00.

Bermuda. 1793. Penny. Extremely fine. Light olive. .75.

Bahama. Halfpenny. Ship sailing. Uncirculated. Brown. .50.

Bulgaria. 1879-1887. 10 Centimes. Uncirculated. Set of 5 pieces. .50.

Byzantine (Constantinople before the Turkish occupation). Cup-shaped. Fine. 1.00 Good. .50.

Congo Free States. 1, 2, 5, 10 Centimes. Round hole in centre. Uncirculated. Bright red. Set for .35.

Cambodia. Norodom I. 1860. 5, 10 Centesimos. Beautiful proofs. .50.

Cyprus. 1, ½, ¼ Piastre. Uncirculated. Bright red. 1.00.

Ceylon. 1815. ½, 1, 2 Stivers. Elephant. Very good and fine. 2.00.

Carthagena. Indian under tree. ¼, 2 R. Very good. .75.

Cape of Good Hope. 1889. Penny. Brilliant proof. .50.

Caracas. ¼ R. Very fine. .25.

Caucasus. Native rulers. 1719. Elephant. Bisti. Very good. 1.00.

Dominica. 1848. ¼ R. Very fine. .25.

Dominica. 1877. Centavo. Uncirculated. .25.

Dominica. 1877. 2½ Centavos. Nickel. Proof. .25.

Dutch East Indies. 6 St. 4¾ inches long. VI—St at each end on both sides. Very fine. Excessively rare. 15.00.

Dutch East Indies. 4¼ St. Over two inches long. Thick. Monogram of the
Dutch East India Co. and 4¼ St. on each side. Very fine. Excessively
rare. 10.00.
England. 1675. Carolus A Carolo. Farthing. Fine. .50. Good. .25.
1680. Charles II. Halfpenny for Ireland. Good. .25.
1714. Anne. Farthing. Bust; rev., Britannia seated, 1714. Uncirculated. Glossy
light brown color. 15.00.
Geo. III. 1797. Twopenny. Weight 2 oz. Uncirculated. 2.50. Fine. 1.50.
Good. 1.00. Fair. .50.
1796 Geo. III. Penny. Weight 1 oz. Uncirculated. 1.50.
1847. Victoria. ½ Farthing. Uncirculated. Bright red. .20.
1793. Coventry Halfpenny. Lady Godiva; rev., elephant. Fine. .75. Good. .50.
1794. Similar; rev., clock tower. Fine. .50.
1795. Similar; rev., elephant. Extremely rare. Not in Conder. Very fine. Light
brown. 5.00.
Ecuador. 1872. 1, 2 Centavos. Very good. Rare. 1.50.
Ecuador. 1884. ½, 1 Centavos. Nickel. Very rare. Very fine pair. 2.50.
France. Henry III. Double Tournois. Fine. .35.
Guatemala. 1871. Centavo. Mountain peaks. Good. .50.

Greece. Head. 1, 2, 5, 10 Lepta. Uncirculated. Bright red. 1.00.
Guiana (Spanish). Lion; rev., castle. Very good. Rude. .50.
Georgia. 1717-1724. Nawiz III. Bisti. Peacock. Very good. Rare. 1.50.
Guernsey. 1, 2, 4, 8 Doubles. 1889. Uncirculated. Bright red. .50.
Griquatown (South Africa). 1890. Penny. Br. proof. .25.
Hayti. 1877. Mercury head. 20 Cent. Proof. .25.
Hong Kong. Cent and Mil. Uncirculated. Bright. .30.
Island of Sumatra. Fine. .25.
Ionian Isles. ¼, ½, 1, 2 Obolo. Fine set. 2.00.
Isle of Man. 1733. Eagle and cradle. This and the following have the three
legs joined on reverse. Very good. .50.
1786. George III. Penny and Halfpenny. Fine. .75.
1813. Head of Geo. III. Uncirculated. Light olive. 1.50. Nearly as choice. 1.00.
Island of Ceylon. Vidschaya Bahu II. 1186-1187. Same. Massa. Very fine. 1.00.
Bhuvanaika Bahu. 1296-1314. Same. Massa. Very fine. 1.00.
Ireland. Gun Money of James II. A remarkably large collection, containing nearly
all the varieties. In condition from fair to about uncirculated; many are
very fine, the best a former owner could find out of hundreds examined.
Half Crowns. 1689: Jan., Mar., July, Aug., Sep., Dec. 1690: Apr., May
(large and small), July. 1690: King on horseback. Shillings. 1689:
Jan., Feb., Mar., July, Aug., Aug't, Sep'r, Sep't, 9. Oct, 10, Nov., Dec.
1690: Apr., May, may, June, Sep. Sixpences. 1689: Jan., Feb., June,
July, Aug., Sep'r, 7ber, Dec. 37 pieces. 25.00.
Java. ½ St. Fine. .35.
Java. 1 Stiver. Without date. Thick dump. Fine. .75.

Java. 1802. 2 Stubers. Oblong bar. Very good. 1.50.
Java. 1818. 2 Stubers. Oblong bar. Very good. 1.50.
Jamaica. Penny and Halfpenny. Alligator above shield. Nickel. Very good. .35.
Japan. Tempo. Oblong. (See cut.) Fine. .15.
Liberia. 1833. Negro, tree and ship. Uncirculated. Brown. .50.
Liberia. 1847. Cent. Palm tree. Extremely fine. .50. Good. .25.
Liberia. 1862. Cent and Two Cents. Uncirculated. 1.25. Another pair, fine. .75.
Liberia. 1862. Two Cents. Proof. 1.25. Extremely fine. .50.
Monaco. 1838. 5, 10 Centimes. Br. proof. .50.
Malacca. 1250. "Cock of the Walk" (See cut). Very fine. .35.
Meysore. Elephant. Thick dump. 5 Cash. Very fine. .50.
Meysore. Lion. Thick dump. 20 Cash. Very fine. .75.
Mexico. Chihuahua. 1860. Liberty seated. ¼ R. Very good. .50.
Chihuahua. 1846. ¼ R. Indian. Fine. .60. Very good. .35.
Jalisco. ¼, ⅛ R. Female with flag. Good. 1.00.
Sinaloa. Head of Liberty. ¼ R. Fine. .50. Good. .25.
Sonora. Female with flag. Cuartilla. Very good. .75.
Zacatecas. Quartilla. Temple and angel. Almost uncirculated. 1.50. Very good.
    1.00.
Zacatecas. · Octavo. Temple and angel. Very good. 1.00.
Guanaxuati. 1856. Cuartilla. Fine and rare. 1.00.
Mexico. 1864. Centavo of Maxmilian. Fine. 1.00. Good. .50.
Nicaragua. 1887. 2 Cents. Br. proof. .25.
Orange Free States. 1888. Penny. Brilliant proof. .35.
Persia. Fath Ali Schah. 1797–1834. 1½ Bisti. Rabbit. Very good. 1.00.
Same ruler. 1½ Bisti. Sun-lion. Fine. 1.00.
Portugal. Maria II. 5 Reis. Uncirculated. Bright red. .25.
Patagonia. Orille-Antoine I. 1874. 2 Centavos. Proof. .25.
Portuguese Africa. ½, 1 Macuta. Very fine. 1 25.
Papal States. Pius IX. 4 Soldi. Bright. .50. Extra fine, olive. .35.
Papal States. Gregory XVI. and Pius IX. Baiocco. Uncirculated. Bright. .75.
Poland. 1831. 3 Grosze. Uncirculated. Brilliant red. .25.
Roman Republic. 40, 4 Baiocchi. Base silver. Very fine and uncirculated. 1.50.
Roman Republic. 3 Baiocchi. Uncirculated. Bright red. 1.00.
Roumania. 5, 10 Bani. Extremely fine. .50.
Russia. 1775–1805. 5 Kopecs. Weight, 2 oz. Very fine. .50. Good. .35.
Sierra Leone. Prowling lion. 1791. Cent. Bronze proof. 1.00.
Sarawak. Cent. Bright. 1.00. Fine. .50.
Sandwich Islands. Kamehameha III. Hapi Haneri. Uncirculated. Bright red.
    .75. Fine. .50.
Siberia. 1764. Set of 10, 5, 3, 2, 1, ½ Kopec, the latter (usually catalogued as ¼
    Kopec) very scarce. All with Sable Foxes except the ½ Kopec. Very
    fine. 7.50.
Siberia. 1796. Magnificent set of rare patterns. Obverse, crowned monogram of
    the emperor surrounded by raised dots denoting the value—a Russian device
    to help the illiterate. 10, 5, 4, 2, 1, ½, ¼ Kopec, with edge varieties of 5,
    4 and 2 Kopecs. The 10 kopec of this set is larger than that with the sable
    foxes. Beautiful brilliant red, or handsomer light bronze proofs. 10 pcs.
    15.00.
South Africa. 1890. Penny. Br. proof. .25.
Suriname. 1764. Coffee plant. About uncirculated. 1.00.
Sweden. Large Or. Size 30. 1685. Fine. 1.00.
States of Jersey. 1888. 1–12, 1–24 Sh. Uncirculated. Bright red. .35.
Sicily. 1849. Ferd. II. ½, 1, 2 Tornese. Uncirculated. Bright red. .75.
Sicily under Napoleon. Head of Jerome Napoleon. 3 Grana. Good. .75.
Strasburg. Siege Decime. 1814–1815. L and N crowned. Fine. Pair. .75.
St. Helena. Halfpenny. Very good. .20.
Augsburg, Brunswick, Rostock, Anhalt, Achen, Mecklenburg, Henneburg, Hamm,

Nassau, Hohenzollern, Lippe, Hesse-Darmstadt, Saxe-Meiningen, Olden-
burg, etc.   Some in 1600.   Bear, Griffin, Horse, Ox-head, Lion, Hen,
Snipe, Pine-cone, Rose, Wheel, etc.   All different.   A very fine lot, 25
uncirculated.   180 pieces.   15.00.

War Medals.

United States.   Silver medal presented to John Bowen, by City of New York
for the war with Mexico.   Arms of New York, rev., typical female pointing to city and harbor—Cerro Gordo—Chapultepec—Cherubusco—Vera
Cruz.   Very fine.   Size 32.   Weight 2 oz. Av.   6.00.

Silver medal presented by South Carolina to Palmetto Regiment, Mexican War.
Palmetto tree; rev., troops landing from boats.   Silver, ribbon attached.
Very fine.   Size 31.   7.50.

Same.   Tin, ribbon attached.   Very fine.   2.00.

Shield shaped badge.   Wreath enclosing cactus, fort, "Mexico 1846;" above, ship,
arms and cannon, names of battles around edge.   Unused.   Bronze.   Size 33
x36.   5.00.

"Death to traitors;" medal of the Iron Brigade, N. Y. Vol's; white metal, ribbon
attached.   Good.   Size 24.   1.00.

West Virginia.   Liberty crowning a soldier, 1861–1865.   Copper.   Uncirculated.
3.00.   Very good.   1.50.

Austria.   Maltese cross for 25 years service, F. W. III. under crown in centre ;
rev., XXV in centre; gilt, ribbon attached.   Size 24.   Perfect.   2.00.

Anhalt.   Shield of arms crowned ; rev., bear walking on wall.   Order of "Albert
the Bear," bronze proof.   Size 20.   1.25.

England.   Waterloo medal.   Bust of Prince Regent ; rev., Victory seated, "Wellington" above, "Waterloo, June 18, 1815" below.   Silver, light scratches on
obverse, ribbon attached.   5.00.

The following English medals all have head of Victoria on obverse and are silver of size 24 unless
otherwise described.

"Ava."   Rev., Victory seated ; "To the Army of India, 1799–1826."   Bar, "Ava,"
ribbon attached.   Very fine.   5.00.

Army of Punjab.   Rev., soldiers surrendering to mounted British officers.   1849.
Two bars, "Mooltan and Goojerat," ribbon attached.   Very fine.   6.00.

"Northwest Frontier."   Rev., Victory crowning a naked warrior.   Bar, "Northwest Frontier," ribbon attached.   Very fine.   5.00.

"Pegu."   Same reverse.   Bar, "Pegu."   Very fine.   3.50.

"Umbeyla."   Same reverse.   Bar, "Umbeyla."   Very fine.   5.00.

Crimea.   Four bars.   "Alma, Balaklava, Inkermann, Sebastapol," ribbon attached.
Very fine.   15.00.

Crimea.   Rev., flying Victory placing wreath on warrior in Roman costume,
"Crimea" in field.   Three bars, "Sebastopol, Inkermann, Alma," ribbon
attached.   Very fine.   10.00.

Same.   One bar, "Sebastopol," ribbon attached, very fine.   4.00.   Another without
bar but with swivel and ribbon, very fine.   3.00.   Another, no bar or ribbon, very fine.   2.50.

India, 1857–58.   Rev., Una and the lion.   Bar, "Delhi," ribbon attached.   Semi-
proof.   Rare.   6.00.

India, 1857–58.   Same reverse.   Bar, Lucknow.   Very fine.   4.00.

India, 1857–58.   Same reverse.   Swivel and ribbon.   Very fine.   3.00.

India, 1857–58.   Same reverse.   Bar, "Central India."   Very fine.   4.00.

India, 1857–58.   Same reverse.   Two bars, "Lucknow," "Defense of Lucknow,"
ribbon attached.   Fine.   6.00.

Baltic, 1854–55.   Rev., Britannia seated, two fortresses in background.   Bar and
ribbon.   Proof.   3.50.

China.   Rev., trophy of arms, flags, etc., "China" below.   Two bars, "Pekin 1860
and Taku Forts 1860," ribbon attached.   Fine.   5.00.

South Africa. Rev., Lion and bush, "South Africa" above. Bar, "1879," ribbon attached. Very fine. 3.50.

Arctic Discoveries. Rev., Arctic scene, 1818–1855. Octagon; ribbon attached. Very fine. Size 22. Rare. 4.00.

1848. Rev., Victory crowning Wellington, "To the British Army, 1793–1814." Bar, "Badajoz," ribbon attached. Very fine. Rare. 6.00.

New Zealand. Head crowned, veil falling down behind; rev., wreath, "New Zealand Virtutis Honor." Ornamented bar and ribbon. Very fine. 4.00.

Abyssinia. Crowned and veiled head in centre of large star, between the points, "Abyssinia;" rev., name of wearer in wreath. Crown and ring with ribbon above. Semi-proof. Size 22. 5.00.

Veiled head of Victoria; rev., a number of semi-nude Ashantees fighting in bush with infantry. Bar and ribbon. Very fine. 3.50.

Egypt. Soudan. Bust of Queen; rev., sphinx. Bar, "El-teb-tamaai," ribbon attached. Fine proof. 6.00.

Egypt. Same design. Bar, "The Nile, 1884–85," ribbon attached. Fine proof. 6.00.

Egypt. Same design. Bar, "Suakim, 1885." Proof. 6.00.

Egypt. Same design. Bar, "Tel-el-kebir," ribbon attached. Fine proof. 6.00.

Bust of Queen; rev., sphinx, 1882, Egypt. Bar, "Tel-el-kebir," ribbon attached. Officers' medal. Semi-proof. Size 12. 3.00.

Afghanistan. Rev., elephant artillery. Bar "Ali Musjid," ribbon attached. Semi-proof. 6.00. Another, plain bar, with ribbon. Proof. 4.00.

Afghanistan. Same design. Bar, "Ahmed Khel," ribbon attached. Fine proof. 6.00.

Persia. Rev., Victory crowning Roman warrior. Bar, "Persia." Fine proof. 6.00.

Sutlej Campaign. Rev., Victory standing holding wreath, war trophies at her feet, Moodkee, 1845, below. Three bars, "Sobraon, Aliwal, Ferozeshuhur." Proof. 10.00.

Syria. 1848. Rev., Britannia seated on hippocampus. Bar, "Syria," ribbon attached. Brilliant proof. 6.00.

Coat of Arms; rev., "For long service and good conduct." Bar with ribbon. Proof. 4.00.

Star of five points, in centre sphinx and pyramids, "Egypt 1882." Rev., crowned monogram. Bar with star and crescent, ribbon attached. Given to English soldiers who served during the war against Arabi Pasha. Perfect. Bronze. Size 30. 3.50.

France. Napoleon III. Expedition to China, 1860. Head. Rev., names of battles. Ribbon with Chinese characters attached. Silver. Size 20. Unused. 3.50.

Same. Officers' size. With ribbon. Unused. Size 11. 2.50.

Same. Unused. Size 7. 1.50.

Napoleon III. For Mexican campaign. 1862–1863. Silver. Very fine. Ribbon attached. Size 20. 2.50.

Republic. Expedition to China, 1883–1885. Rev., names of battles. Silver. Size 20. Unused. 3.00.

Prussia. 1870–1871. W. crowned. Gilt. Very fine. Size 19. .35.

Saxe-Gotha-Altenburg. The Altenburg rose; rev., ducal crown. Bronze. Very fine. Size 27. 1.00.

Turkey. For Crimea, 1855. Trophy of cannon, etc.; rev., cipher of Abdul Medjid. Silver. Size 24. Very fine. 2.00.

Numismatic Books and Pamphlets.

Steigerwalt's Illustrated History of United States and Colonial Coins. Many illustrations and the cheapest work of its class. Cloth. .75. Stiff paper covers, .50.

"Early Half Dimes," Harold P. Newlin, 1883. Full descriptions of the varieties of the early dates and also an interesting article on the whereabouts of all the known 1802 Half Dimes. Fine paper with broad margins. New. Edi-

tion very limited. Illustrated with plates. Cloth, 1.00. Paper (no pl
reduced to .25.

Madden's History of Jewish coinages. Many illustrations. 350 pages. Half
rocco. New and uncut. 5.00.

Atlas Numismatique du Canada. Jos. Le Roux. 1883. 40 pages, with illustra
of all the 220 Canadian coins. Letter press in English and French,
valuable work. Paper covers. 1.00.

Coin Collectors' Manual. Jones. 1860. .50.

Silver coins of England. Henry. 1878. 48 pages. Illustrated pamphlet.

Numisgraphics or a list of sale catalogues. Atinnelli, 1876. 134 pages. P
covers. Rare. 2.00.

Haseltine's "Paper Money of the Colonies." Illustrated. Pamphlet. 5 pl
Reduced to .15.

Haseltine's "Confederate Notes and Bonds." .25.

"Das Romische Ass." German. 24 pages. 6 plates. .35.

The Naturalist's Directory. Cassino. 1886. 4801 names. 1.00.

Coins, medals and seals. W. C. Prime. 114 plates. 292 pages. Cloth.
York, 1861. 3.50.

Silver coins of England. Hawkins. 308 pages. 47 plates. Half Morocco.
don. 1841. 3.50.

Coins of the Grand Master of Malta. R. Morris, Boston, 1884. 6 plates. 70 pa
Cloth. 1.50.

The coinage of Morelos. Illustrated 4to. pamphlet. Lyman Low. Priva
printed. 18 pages. N. Y., 1886. .50.

American Journal of Numismatics. Vol. 1 to Vol. 9, No. 1 bound in two v
one half, and the other full morocco. Vol. 9, No. 2 to Vol. 14, (excep
13 No. 4, and 14 No. 4), Vol. 17, 18, 19, No. 1 and 2, unbound. The
missing numbers, Vol. 15 and 16, and late issues (now in 25th Vol.), ca
supplied, if desired, at $2 per Vol. to complete set. 25.00.

Le Medaillier Du Canada. Jos. LeRoux, Montreal. 1888. Cloth with additi
paper supplement. Illustrates over 1800 Canadian coins and medals. 6

Descriptive Catalogue of the Seavey Collection owned by Loring G. Parme
Cambridge. 1873. 63 pages. 4 plates. Half morocco. Issued at 3
1.50.

Historia Numorum. A Manual of Greek Numismatics by Barclay V. Head, Assis
Keeper of the Department of Coins and Medals in the British Muse
1887. Hundreds of illustrations. 818 pages. Half morocco. By far
best work of its class ever issued. 12.50.

The Coinages of the World. G. D. Mathews. Profusely illustrated. 8vo. Cl
New York, 1876. 3.00.

New Varieties of Gold and Silver Coins, etc. Eckfeldt and Dubois. Phila., 1
Covers loose. Illustrated. Contains about 50 to 75 cts. worth of real g
fastened to page 45 illustrating metals. 1.50.

"Early Coins of America," by S. S. Crosby. 331 pages. 12 heliotype plates
110 fine cuts, large quarto. In parts as originally issued. 6.00.

Marvin's Masonic Medals. 17 plates. Also, accurate descriptions of 744 med
Heavy paper. The standard American publication. 350 pages. N
10.00.

Curiosities.

Knight of Pythias sword. Handsome steel scabbard and mountings. Knights,
grims, Eagles, etc. Very fine and desirable. Probably made for an off
and cost about $30. Uninjured by use. In buckskin cover. 10.00.

A single hair from the head of Henry Clay. Taken when the body was lying
state at Baltimore. .50.

Massive brown agate paper weight, in shape of a seal and handle, cut from
piece. Very handsome and valuable. 5¾ inches long, 2¾ inches w
at top. 5.00.

Seal. Similar. Red agate. 2⅛ inches long. Handsome. 2.50.

Marble paper weight. "Appian Way," near Ravenna, Italy. .75.

Bohemian glass, beads and specimens of. 20 pieces. Lot for 1.00.

Egyptian scarabeus. Very fine. 1.50.

Olive wood pipe. Liberty bell design. New. .50.

Japan. Native painted photo. on glass in case. Very odd. 1.00.

Japan. Opium pipe. New. .75.

Piece of gold ore, oval, polished ready for mounting as a breast pin. Size 26. 5.00.

Aztec Idol, carved from pumice stone, prehistoric, very fine specimen, dug from mound near Durango, Mexico. 15x9x7 inches. Very desirable. 100.00.

Hindoo Idol. Fine white marble. Old. 16 x 9½ in. 25.00.

Old Japanese. God of Plenty. Very odd. Bronze. 6 x 4 in. 10.00.

Old Japanese. Dog Foy on stump. Bronze. 4 x 4 in. 10.00.

Agate egg. Full size of a hen's egg. Very handsome. 1.50.

Paper weight. Glass. View of foreign building. 3 inches. .50.

Agatized wood, partially coated with amethyst crystals. Cross section of tree. One face polished, the other rough. 6x7 in. 3 in. thick. Beautiful specimen, the polishing alone cost nearly $10. 7.50.

Jasperized wood, shows the bark distinctly. Cross section of tree. One side polished, the other rough. 7x8 in. 2 in. thick. As handsome as last. 7.50.

Ostrich egg. South Africa. Fine large specimen. 2.50.

Fine specimen of amber with insect enclosed. Rare. 1.50. Smaller. 1.00.

Silver female, Peruvian figure with long hair. Hung, with prayer, on the figure of the 'Virgin for the cure of disease. 1¾ inches. Rare. 2.00.

Indian doe-skin slipper. Fancy bead work. Very fine. 1.00.

Pottery vase and ball stopper from Cyprus. Old and valuable. 2.00.

Small wooden figure of elephant, ivory tusks, 2½ in. 1.50.

Ivory queen, black, elaborately carved dress. 3.00.

Ancient bronze statuette. Venus. 2½ in. From Syria. 3.00.

Ancient bronze statuette. Curious animal. 1½ in. From Syria. 2.00.

Ancient Roman spearhead, iron, 3½ in. From German Mound. 2.00.

Terra Vert Ancient Egyptian ornaments, Lion, Anubias, etc. 5 pcs. Lot for 7.50.

Plumes of the Egret or White Crane, snow white, 22 in., Florida. 2.00.

Skin of Mottled Crane, very fine, 27 in., Florida. 1.50.

Curious polished stone, natural scene resembling a river and bank with trees and foliage. 10½ in. 5.00.

Remarkable clay idol from Guatemala. Human figure with tail. Head broken from body (has been mended), and part of legs missing. Curious and rare. 2.50.

Florida sea-beans. 14 pcs. .75.

Beautiful polished section of elephant tusk. 5¼x6 in. 3.50.

Gourd Dish. From Peruvian mound. Fine. 1.00.

Brazil. Nut-case filled with nuts. 4x4. 2.00.

Curious bark writing in native India characters, 3 fine specimens, and a piece of tappa cloth. 4 pcs. 1.00.

Pair of very old galoshes. 1.50.

Handsome polished tiger-eye ball, suitable for cane or umbrella handle. 1¼ in. in diameter. 1.00.

Remarkable old mortar and pestle. The mortar is dated 1694, and has odd dragon head handles. 10.00.

Pair of handles from very old desk, ram's head with ring in mouth. Bronze. 1.00.

Apache horn spoon. 9 in. in length. 4 in. wide. 1.50.

Wooden vases. 5½ in. high. Made from the Great Elm on Boston Common. 2 pcs. 1.00.

Geode, Ill. 4½ in. wide, 2 in. high. Nice specimen. 1.50.

Amethyst crystals. Hungary. 4x3½ in. 1.50.

Peacock Brass Incense Burner. 14 in. high. Beautifully carved with Persian figures. A rare Persian ornament. 15.00.

Bowl. Brass. Persia. A beautiful, rare and valuable specimen. 10 in. in diameter, 6 in. deep. The sides beautifully ornamented with procession of 12 odd figures of priests and animals. 10.00.

Mounted lens (2), each 2 in., on stand. 1.00.

Olive wood seal top. .25.

Brass spoon mould. Very old. 7¾ in. 2.00.

Lock and flint from old pistol. .25.

Fine specimen of opal in matrix. Mexico. 1.50.

Gold ore, oval polished specimens, once set in sleeve-buttons, contain considerable gold. Size 9. 4 pcs. 5.00.

Curious match-safe, form of beetle. 4 in. .50.

Brass candlesticks. Assortment of designs, all polished. 43 pcs. 15 00.

Brass candlestick, snuffers and tray, polished. Old and desirable. 3.50.

Very old paper-snapper, brass dragon. 5 in. 1.00.

Bone spoons, very old, 6 inches. 4 pcs. 1.50.

Bone two-pronged fork, very old. 6½ in. 1.00.

Very old powder-flask. 2.00.

Very old knife, four broad blades, three with crescent projections to cut button-holes, handle about 1½ inch at bottom and only ½ inch at top. Curious. 2.50.

Very old wooden spoon, large bowl, elaborately carved handle; evidently a high-priced soup-spoon. 9 in. 1.50.

Beautiful necklace of 50 handsome large Brazilian agate beads, finely matched in size and markings. 5.00.

Patrick Henry. A very fine bust of bronzed zinc. 14 inches high. 5.00.

Curious carved ivory clenched hands (tops of old seals). 4 pcs. 2.00.

South Sea Islander's wooden spear. In two pieces (made that way). 32 inches. 1.50.

Small figure of Napoleon, lead, very old. .50.

Ivory chessmen from Siam. Old. 3 pcs. 1.50.

Egypt. Goddess of Evil, Taur. 3500 years old. Hyena-headed goddess with big feet. Fine. 2⅜ inches. Very rare. 10.00.

Antique lamp, Roman, of the kind used in Biblical times. Very fine specimen. 5.00.

Collection of Proof Sets.

1859-1890. A collection of 33 Proof Sets, inclusive of both sets of 1873 ("Old" and "New" style) in choice condition. Cheap at 140.00.

Collection of War Cards and Tokens.

A splendid collection of War Cards and Tokens formed by the former owner at the period and struck to his order. The collection (so marked) contains 24 silver, 470 nickel and about 500 copper—all different (about 1000)—and there are over 300 in addition (100 nickel) that may be part of the collection, but have not had time to compare to ascertain. The silver cards are rare, and the large collection of nickel cards, *all brilliant proofs*, could not be equalled; the copper cards and tokens are also proofs or uncirculated. A valuable collection. 1335 pcs. 50.00.

Paper cutter. Brass. India. Double god at end. 9½ inches. 2.50.

Whale's tooth. Polished specimen. 6¾ in. 2.00.

Hammer. Walrus tusk head. 1.00.

Marline spike. Walrus tusk. 12 in. 1.50.

A magnificent pair of walrus tusks, each 18 inches long, beautifully carved the whole length, one touched up with colored ink. One has a deer, a mermaid, a girl, a woman, the other has a sailor carrying rescued woman; lady reading letter, American flag and eagle above; sailor's monument 15.00.